An Anthology for the Adult Reader

INDIAN TALES OF NORTH AMERICA

EDITED BY TRISTRAM P. COFFIN

American Folklore Society, Inc.
Philadelphia, Pa. 1961

Bibliographical and Special Series, vol. 13

International Standard Book Number 0-292-73506-5
Library of Congress Catalog Card Number 61-11866
Copyright © 1961 by the American Folklore Society
All rights reserved
Printed in the United States of America

Sixth Printing, 1975

to

Rusty
Pat, Mark, Ricki, Jock

PREFACE

The tales that follow were edited by a folklorist trained in the history of literature. Clearly, the presentation is not that of the anthropologist with his interest in the ethnological, psychological, and sociological role of narrative art. Rather, it is that of the *littérateur* using the admittedly ethnocentric and artificial point of view of the intelligent, curious Western European reader.

The anthropologist using this book for classwork and the scholar particularly interested in the subject of North American Indian narrative will want to supplement the "Remarks on Reading the Tales" with Franz Boas essays in *Race, Language, and Culture* (New York, 1940), with Paul Radin's study of *The Trickster* (London, 1955), and with Radin's "Literary Aspects of North American Mythology" in the *Geological Survey of Canada, Museum Bulletin 16, Anthropological Series 6, 1-51* (Ottawa, 1915), as well as with the more specialized studies of Morris E. Opler on the Apache and Melville Jacobs on the Clackamas Chinook. Excellent sources for such bibliography lie in the "1947 Report of the Committee on Research in Folklore" in *Folklore Research in North America* (Journal of American Folklore, 1947, 350-416) and in the yet-to-be-published article that William Fenton has done for the *Encyclopaedia Britannica*. For the reader who simply wants to pursue the subject further, the final pages of this book include a listing of other collections of North American Indian tales published by the American Folklore Society. In addition, one can turn to Stith Thompson's classic anthology and analysis, *Tales of the North American Indians*, (Cambridge, 1929). This book contains many stories not given in the present volume, copious comparative notes, maps, and detailed bibliographies for further reading. There is also a bibliography in the back of Thompson's *The Folktale* (New York, 1946) that lists collections that have appeared in the following periodicals and series: *Anthropological Papers of the American Museum of Natural History, New York; Anthropological Series of the Field Museum of Natural History; Anthropological Series of the Geological Survey of Canada; Bulletin of the Bureau of American Ethnology; Bulletin of the American Museum of Natural History, New York; Columbia University Contributions to Anthropology; Publications in Anthropology, University of Washington; Publications of the American Ethnological Society; Publications of the*

Carnegie Institution; Publications of the Jessup North Pacific Expedition; Report of the Bureau of American Ethnology; University of California Publications in American Archaeology and Ethnology; University Museum Anthropological Publications, University of Pennsylvania.

Of course, the present volume attempts something that none of the above-mentioned books and articles has attempted ---that is, to present North American Indian Tales as stories that are "simply worth reading". This cardinal fact must be remembered by all who use the book.

In the way of acknowledgements, I am particularly grateful to Horace P. Beck, William Fenton, MacEdward Leach, and Thomas Lowry for suggestions, time, and encouragement. I also want to mention G. Wallace Chessman, whose enthusiasm for the material at a long-forgotten dinner party started me toward assembling the present anthology.

T. P. Coffin
Wakefield, R. I.
November 1960

CONTENTS

REMARKS ON READING THE TALES

North American Indian tales are usually published in one of two ways: either in hard-to-come-by scholarly works, where they are analyzed and classified; or in children's collections, where they are sentimentalized and emasculated. Thus, the intelligent adult reader seldom gets the opportunity to enjoy and profit from one of the richest literary traditions in the human heritage. This book, which is not for scholars and not for children, is designed to introduce its reader to some of the best of the North American Indian tales. The pages that follow offer much good reading. Each of the selections has withstood the toughest test to which art can be subjected -- oral tradition, where what fails to please is simply forgotten through disuse, and what pleases is repeated, varied, and fostered by generation after generation. The tales may be enjoyed at this level alone. However, they offer a great deal more than mere pleasure. They offer the reader a glimpse at raw genius, untutored, unsubtle, as it goes directly about the task of explaining the world and man's duties in it. As one reads the tales, he will be refreshed by a simple faith in creation and an enjoyment of life that the technologically superior modern world recalls little of.

In the pages that follow, one quickly learns that the primitive mind is incapable of the subtleties and probings we have come to expect of our own narrators. Thus, some explanation of the vast differences in the way an Indian tells a story and in the way a civilized man tells a story is in order. The remarks below are divided into two main parts: one, a treatment of the specific differences in narrative technique; two, a discussion of the basic attitude toward life that lies behind the tales.

The following statements concerning plot, setting, character, and purpose in Indian and literary narratives can be made. The Indian tale begins in a leisurely fashion and repeats itself regularly as an integral part of its nature. The literary tale begins rapidly (usually attempting to arouse curiousity at once) and shuns repetition. The plot of the Indian tale tends toward simplicity, with little use of sub-plotting or variety. Invariably, the Indian tale is simple in its use of characterization and setting. Characters are black and white, only such qualities as directly affect the story are mentioned, and seldom do more than two persons act in a scene at one time. Settings are general and have no real interplay with the events or characters of the plot. On the other hand, the literary author frequently subordinates all to characterization, usually attempts to go beneath the surface to probe motivation and reaction, and frequently uses setting as an active force in moving plot and developing character. The Indian tale's purpose is clearly to entertain and to maintain the ways of the group. The literary tale must also entertain, but that it makes more than a casual attempt at preserving the ways of our culture is doubtful.

It is clear then that what the reader will learn to appreciate in the literature of the Indian does not center on characterization and setting, but rather on the action and on the way life is observed. Let's consider the action or plot first.

The stories of the world, literary and folk, divide themselves into four main classes according to plot: the single incident; the string of incidents; the Aristotelian unified plot, with its beginning, middle, and end; and the meaningful vignette plot. Most of us are quite familiar with all these forms. The single incident can be illustrated by a glimpse at "Eye-Juggler" story on page 146 or at the "Turtle's Sacred War-Bundle" story on page 149. This type of narration is also the usual form of the anecdote and the dirty joke. The single incident is obviously the simplest form a tale can take. Because it needs no pattern of organization, no characterization, or real setting, it can spring up even in the most naive of minds. However, when a series of these single incidents are linked together extremely long and complicated tales may result. It is through such linkages that the usual plot of the folk seems to have grown. Tales such as those involving the adventures of Coyote, Whiskey Jack, and Naniboju are good illustrations of the series of incidents plot. In fact, it would not be surprising to find almost all the trickster incidents included in this book joined together into one long account told by some Indian informant. Such stories are of course no more than a chain of events. There is no overall unity that demands what order the various incidents must take, nor does it really matter whether incidents are subtracted or added in the beginning, middle, or end, for in no absolute sense does a beginning, a middle, and an end exist. Naturally, certain performers and groups have their preferences. We must be aware that for each narrator and for each set of listeners there is an integrity of plot and of plot organization, and that the incorporation of additional elements or the omission of expected elements is resisted.

The folk as a whole, and the primitive Indian particularly, are not capable of unifying their tales in the fashion described by

Aristotle when he observed Graecian drama and illustrated by Homer when he arranged *The Odyssey*. Such unification is the product of a high degree of civilization. Of course, fairy tales, beast stories, and other material developed in a civilized area such as medieval Europe or Hindu India might find their way into the repetoire of the primitive narrator as he makes contact with higher levels of civilization. The Jesuits in the New World introduced the Indian to hundreds of European and Asian stories that reflect a knowledge on the part of their authors of Graecian plot unity. But one cannot expect more than the series of incidents plot in pre-Columbian Indian material such as that included in this book.

One must be careful before he judges stories too harshly for lacking plot unity. While we today might consider such stories as crude and lacking in true form, we have to keep in mind that much of our classical European literature, coming in the times when the Greek-Roman tradition had been obscured, falls back into methods of plot organization close to the series of incidents type. The medieval romances are a good case in point. In fact, most of the writers who wrote in Europe after the Fall of Rome and before the Renaissance do not handle plot well in the Aristotelian sense. In England, Chaucer's *Troilus and Criseyde* stands as a landmark partly because of its tight unity. And, although *Beowulf*, *Sir Gawain and the Green Knight*, and a few other poems show a definite awareness on the part of their writers of Aristotelian principles of construction, generally it is safe to say that the unified plot is one of the things the Renaissance brought back to Western culture.

The 20th Century has of course revolted against the strictness and artificialities of the beginning, middle, and end type of plot. Today, we prefer a story that is as realistic as life itself, a tale that begins nowhere in particular and ends nowhere in particular, but that is tightly organized around characterization. These vignettes strive for extreme realism and utilize our modern knowledge of the sub-conscious, hidden motivation, and behaviour patterns. Checkov, Katherine Mansfield, Virginia Woolf are three acknowledged masters of this method.

Therefore, it is clear that if we are to enjoy or profit from the tales of the Indian, we must take those tales at the level of which their authors were capable, and not demand of them things that simply don't exist in them. While the Indian may have known little about psychology, he followed one principle of story-telling that our modern writers sometimes forget in their eagerness to reveal personality. He knew that the tale is the thing -- and he seldom let anything prevent him from moving swiftly and clearly through a good narrative.

In the literary expression of civilized peoples, logical consistency of time, sequence, detail, and motive is often a fetish. In modern times, novelists, dramatists, movie and television script men have become so conscientious about these matters that they continually sacrifice the pace of their story to make certain no critic will accuse them of an inconsistency or a failure to tie up a loose end. The result is that we have a hugh body of self-conscious, over-disciplined expression in which the main purpose of narrative, telling a good tale, gets lost. Nor is the weakness confined to the poorer writers. It is as common in the Henry James novel where the relationships of character and action are so involved the book becomes a magnificent technical exercise as it is in the musical movie which forgets its central appeal of sex and song to make tediously sure that boy meets, loses, and gets girl. It is evident in the elaborate symbolism and narrative patterns of a Joyce or a Faulkner, in the feverish accuracy of a historical movie or Book-of-the-Month Club novel, even in the stage sets and costumes of a Broadway play. The best works of the best writers succeed in spite of all this, just as Pope wrote successfully under the handicaps of 18th Century verse, but one senses our literature has been victimized by our tremendous scientific and technological advances.

Primitive minds, and so primitive stories, do not concern themselves with scientific, logical accuracy. An Indian tale such as the Southern Paiute "Theft of Fire" text which is printed on page 21 would stagger the modern critic who took it seriously. When one reads this tale, it becomes clear that statements made in the story and that trouble the modern mind are of no concern to the Indian narrator. The people have no fire, but they are able to heat stones. The animals see fire and recognize it, although they have never known it. Fish flies even though he has no wings and doesn't know if he can. The fire is not far off, but none of the birds is able to see it. The animals make fire drills in anticipation of the incredibly astute question they must answer, although they have never had fire. The hosts realize that Coyote and the rest have come to steal fire, although they have no reason in the world for such suspicions. They also watch Coyote's whole deceit aware of what he is going to do, but without attempting to prevent his doing it. Nor is Coyote grateful for his friends' aid; he kills nearly all of them. However, the real point with this tale is not that these inconsistencies exist, but that the story is functioning a-logically, or with a completely different logical system from the one we are used to using. The important thing is *what happened*. The narrator and the listeners know what happened. The flow of the plot is thus inevitable, and events that are *to be* in the narrative can be referred to as *being* and demand no explanations no matter how strange they seem. One cannot change the way in which fire came to the tribe. The script is simply accepted.

Though this way of handling a story may bother the modern reader, it is not unknown to him. Many of the classics of our literature, produced when the authors were closer to the folk than we are today, show similar characteristics. Aeschylus' Clytemnestra knows what has happened at the Fall of Troy before the first Herald has come from the battlefields. Seneca's Thyestes tells his children how he fears for them should they return to Atreus' kingdom, yet he hurries them off to their doom. Shakespeare puts a clock in Julius Caesar's Rome.

Today, the only haven for such "blunders" is in the little nonsense literature we have, where concern with proper technique can be dismissed because of the very nature of the form. Observe any popular cartoon strip, like *L'il Abner, Pogo, or Peanuts*. Their narrative method is remarkably similar to that of the "Theft of Fire" tale, and their absurdities of logic and inconsistencies of action would not seem at all foreign to the folk, even if they occured in serious literature. However, we of recent times are quite firm in our attitude about such matters. We will permit Oscar Wilde to motivate his heroine's love life on her fondness for the name Ernest and we will permit W. S. Gilbert to hang the plot of an operetta on the fact one character threatens to curse another, but we insist on associating a certain triviality with such goings-on.

It is probable we have lost sight of an essential ingredient. We accept conventions in order to have art -- and to exclude a convention as useful as logical inconsistency and scientific inaccuracy may well do our literature great damage in the long run. The freedom of movement, the sharpness of contrast, the speed that we allow in nonsense writing and can observe in tales like these Indian tales could be so useful to our serious writer -- if we would only let him use them.

All this brings us rather naturally to the differences in attitude toward life of the Indian and the modern civilized man. What must be said is subtle and begins with the trite observation that the contemporary is anchorless, without much faith in his ancient religion, and dependent on a science that has been born from his own mind. In a real sense, psychological, sociological, and physical laws are the only things he will trust. The Indian is different. He trusts life itself.

Acceptance of life can best be defined as that unquestioning enthusiasm for society, that zest for the way of the world, which allows certain human beings to embrace the joys and tragedies of everyday living without hesitation or real desire for what is called "improvement". Of course, this acceptance of life is not necessarily a characteristic of the individual; on the contrary, it is an integral part of every age in every culture regardless of technological level. In primitive societies, where man knows nothing more, it is always in the ascendency. In highly civilized groups, for example England of the last 300 years, its influence may rise and fall, as the group pushes onward and upward toward "a better world to live in".

It seems to be the quality John F. Genung expressed when trying to describe Robert Louis Stevenson's attitude toward life.

> If he had the framing of an ideal for us, his first counsel, I imagine, would be Do not assume an attitude toward life at all, but just live; do not be a spectator and critic of the business of living, but throw yourself into the heart of it, and be all there, and say no more about it.

and that Alfred North Whitehead meant when he remarked,

> Shakespeare wrote better poetry for not knowing too much; Milton, I think, knew too much finally for the good of his poetry.

and that Henry Adams had in mind when he stated in *Mont-Saint -Michel and Chartres,*

> Understand, we cannot! nothing proves that the greatest artists who ever lived have, in a logical sense, understood! or that omnipotence has ever understood!

As one thinks further along this line, it appears there may well be a close relationship between religious faith in a culture and acceptance of life. In short, cultures, or parts of cultures,

naive enough to believe fully in their philosophy of life and after-
life are willing to take things as they come; while cultures, such
as our own, where the majority are somewhat skeptical about their
religion tend to struggle with the world they find about them,
hoping, one would suppose, to eventually construct "their heaven
on earth".

The relationship between the stories that people use to explain the mysteries of existence and the ability they possess to
accept life is so close that one is led to suspect that naiveté is
an essential ingredient of the very best artistic expression. Artistic
vitality depends to an immense degree on the certainty of the com-
poser and it is difficult to be sure, in an anchorless and questioning world. Even the agnostic may be startled to find himself be-
lieving firmly that there can be no really great art in a culture
that has no real religious belief.

The tales in this book are, to be sure, permeated with acceptance of the world and faith in the traditional explanations of
the life process. Intensely religious, the Indian read religion into
every facet of existence, into every object, animal, and event that
fell under his scrutiny. He shows no desire to have things ap-
preciably different or to change the world for what might seem
"the better". His tales, as sacred to him as *The Bible* has been
to us, tell him with authority how the world came to be the way
that it is, reveal to him exactly what he must know to adjust to
his environs, and give him a glimpse at the sheer excitement offered by danger and pleasure, evil and good -- in brief, by life
itself.

All the selections in this anthology are mythological; historical accounts, European imports, and explanations of tribal rites
have been excluded. This means that the stories, with one or two
exceptions, are set in an earlier era, when animals, birds, objects,
forces of nature, and the like behaved as human beings behave.
While this concept varies from tribe to tribe, and is lacking to
Eskimo and a few Southwestern groups, it dominates most of the
pages to come. Thus, the hero of any story may seem to be
human at one moment and animal at the next. Coyote can howl
at the moon and build a fire; Eagle can fly about the sky and have
intercourse with a girl. This concept is confusing to the civilized
reader and admittedly is not always clear-cut to the trained anthropologist. But it is a mythological concept and not a happy convention like those of the medieval beast story or the modern cartoon.

Many of the tales obviously serve to account for the way of
life that the Indian knew. The mysteries of nature, the structure

of the Indian social system, the origin of necessities like sexual intercourse and hunting are treated. On the other hand, some of the tales have lost their explanatory nature over the years and now appear only as adventure stories taking place in a by-gone era. The reader will suspect that the tale once had a ritualistic connection, but it is obvious neither he nor the narrator makes any such connection any longer.

A final group of stories, usually referred to as trickster tales, centers around the adventures of a hero who is at one moment a stupid dupe, at the next a clever knave. To confuse the issue further, the trickster may also serve as the religious figure who regulates the world and teaches culture habits to the tribe. Thus about two-thirds of the Indians knew stories of pranks and buffoonery carried on by a character who stands roughly in the same relationship to their religion as Christ does to Christianity. Judged by Christian standards, this trickster may also seem un-ethical, dishonest, and petty. In fact, most often he is on the side of evil. However, the reader must never forget the Indian was originally no Christian. He, like most primitives, was more in-terested in the end than in the means and, providing the job was successfully done, he cared little whether deceit and knavery were used to accomplish it. Nevertheless, as the trickster fails even more often than he succeeds, it seems likely the trickster stories were told to demonstrate for the people what should not be done and to point a moral. At least, the Navaho told trickster tales for such a purpose. It is also interesting to note that many modern Indians, confused by this dual role of the trickster, separate a character like Coyote in his good tales from the Coyote of the bad tales.

Finally, the reader must be warned the stories are not in-tended to be cute, quaint, childish, or even vulgar. They are the ancient and revered legends of a primitive people. That they in-corporate fancy, evil, cruelty, crudity, beauty, and good all at once is because life incorporates these things -- and unlike the Christian the Indian was always true to life in his religious tales. He ac-cepted evil and good, cruelty and beauty, crudity and fancy all equally as part of the way of the world he found about him.

Each selection is taken, with permission, from the *Journal of American Folklore,* a scholarly quarterly that has been published since 1888 by the American Folklore Society. The men and women who collected and originally edited these tales were the leading anthropologists and folklorists of their times. The present editor has remained faithful to their texts, some of which are taken straight from the mouths of bi-lingual natives. The editing that has been done has been directed toward the modification of un-printable words and concepts and in the interests of pace and readability. In one or two cases, clearly marked in the notes, stories that were collected separately but which frequently are found together have been put together. Essentially, though, the tales are just as they appeared when they were published in the *Journal* -- as the collector heard them or as he translated them from an Indian tongue.

It has taken us a long time to realize that we never bothered to understand the Indians or their culture as we claimed, stole, and wheedled the United States and Canada away from them. We saw the Indians as agents of the Devil; we called them sneaky and cowardly; we said they broke treaties. Actually, we were wrong about them. We should have known better had we stopped to un-derstand their religion, their concepts of discretion and courage, their ideas of property and chiefhood. Surely, it is late now to educate ourselves about a great people who are absorbed and ac-culturated. But it is never too late to profit from and enjoy the art they left us far more willingly than they left us their hunting grounds. It is a great art, and it will not take the reader long to realize the tales below have stood the test of time because they are great tales. As a human being, he may respond to them as other human beings did for generation after generation in the lodges and tipis of America's unmolested forests and plains.

Part 1
THE WAY THE WORLD IS

Few North American Indians attempted to account for the act of creation itself, but most of the tribes had myths which tell of the coming of man to the present earth. The most common Indian myth begins with a primeval water, out of which some animal brings up a few grains of sand or mud which a culture hero then develops into the world. Tale 2, The Earthdiver, from the California Western Mono is pretty typical of this story. However, there were a number of peoples in southwestern and southeastern areas, as well as a few Iroquoian tribes near the Great Lakes, who thought of man as first is-suing from a hole in the ground, as in Tale 1, The Emergence. Generally speaking, it is safe to assume that tribes who tell emergence stories do not tell earthdiver stories, although some of the southwestern Apaches united the two concepts. Many of the emergence myths are extremely long and include information concerning the coming of death, sex, and such things into the world. The Hopi text that follows is abbreviated, and we will turn to other tribes for accounts of the coming of death, sex, fire, and the like.

1. THE EMERGENCE

(Hopi)

In the Underworld all the people were fools. Youths copulated with the wives of elder men, and the elder men attacked virgins. All was confusion, and the chief was unhappy. He thought, and at sunset proclaimed that on the next day all the people should assemble around him. On the following morning all came. They said, "We heard you announce, you have sent for us. What do you wish; perhaps you wish to tell us something." "Yes," said the chief, "I want to tell you that I have been thinking much, and I am saddened by your evil ways. Now, I announce that tomorrow morning early, all the women, virgins, and female children and infants, all females, shall remain here in the village, and all the men, youths, and male infants, all males, shall cross the broad river and remain there on the other side." Neither the men or the women were displeased by this announcement, and discussed it overnight. "Now it will be seen who the lazy ones are, perhaps the women, perhaps the men; we will see." On the following morning, the males all swam the river, carrying the infants on their backs, and leaving the women in the houses which belonged to them. Before the men swam the river, the men and women divided all kinds of seeds between them, all the store of seeds was divided.

The men carried their hunting weapons with them and caught deer and antelope. They nursed the infants by cutting up small bits of venison which they gave to the infants to suck, and it was as good as mother's milk. They grew fat and strong. The men built houses and planted, and at the end of one year gathered large harvests. The women had but little skill in field work and only obtained a small harvest. The men came down to the river bank and displayed their abundant field fruits and taunted the women. It was an evil time and both men and women were foolish. When they became amorous they resorted to artificial means to satisfy themselves. The women used sticks and cactus and the men used liver of deer and squashes and gourds. In six moons, one of these gourds gave birth to Gourd Girl, a very beautiful maid. Also during this separation of sexes, a young woman, not a virgin, imitated intercourse by using the primary wing feather of an eagle. She conceived and was carried to the San Francisco Mountains where she gave birth to Giant Eagle, a monster.

Another young woman, not a virgin either, was sitting in her house in great misery. Her body was barely covered, for her gown only hung over her in ragged shreds. She was very lousy and was picking the vermin off and was scratching herself. While she was doing this, almost all of her body was exposed. The rays of the sun coming through a crack in the wall fell upon her. She moved in pleasure; then fell asleep. She told some elder women of this experience. It began to rain, and the water started to drip through the roof. The elder women said to her, "Lie over there and let the raindrops fall upon you." She went over and lay down. The raindrops fell upon her body; again she moved in pleasure and fell asleep. She conceived and gave birth to twins. In four days they were able to walk and run around. They were foolish and full of mischief, breaking and destroying food vessels and cooking utensils. They were very dirty and their noses were always snotty.

When the Twins had grown to be the size of a twelve-year-old boy, they frequently asked their grandmother, Spider Woman, who their father was and where he lived. But Spider Woman would say, "How should I know?" At last, she told them that Sun was their father, that he lived at the place of Sunrise, and she would go with them and they should see him. She perched on the ear of one of the Twins. She spurted some medicine and a filament spread before them, making a smooth pathway to the door of the house of Sun. There sat Lion, Bear, and Rattlesnake; Serpent sat on the hatchway. The Twins successivly spurted medicine upon these watchers as they came to them, saying as they did so, "Our friend, do not be angry," and each watcher in turn lay down quietly, and they passed on and stood looking down the hatchway. There were many beautiful young women and virgins down there. They were the daughters of Sun. Some of them looked up and said, "Who are these dirty, snotty-nosed young ones, I wonder?" The Wife of Sun said, "Come in you two," and they went down the ladder. In the middle of the floor was a mound of turquoise and on its top was a large abalone. This was the seat of Sun. Around the floor were many other smaller turquoise mounds on which were seated the Wife of Sun and his daughters. The Wife of Sun got angry at the Twins. The daughters asked them who they were and where they came from. But the Twins sat in silence. Then the daughters said, "You may sit there, on these two mounds, and be brothers until our father comes home; then we will know." The Sun came home, from the below, coming up a ladder leading through a hatchway in the floor. He always entered with a great noise. As he emerged, he said, "What do I smell? There are some strange ones in here." The daughters had put the Twins away in the cloud altar before Sun came in, and when Sun demanded that the strangers be brought forth, the daughters brought the Twins from the beautiful cloud altar where they had been covered with clouds of all colors. The Twins ran to Sun, claiming him as their father, but Sun said, "Wait a while." Sun brought out his great pipe of turquoise, with clouds painted on the sides. Filling it with tobacco and ramming it with a stick, he lit it and gave it to the Twins, who smoked it, passing it from one to the other. They swallowed the smoke, which now appears as clouds in the sky.

After they had smoked the pipe, the Twins again claimed Sun as their father. But he said, "Wait a while". There was a high mountain, its top almost touching the sky. Sun showed this to the Twins and told them to go to its top and sleep there. Spider Woman tied a turkey feather to the right side of one Twin and another turkey feather to the left side of the other Twin. They went up to the top of the mountain and the wind blew cold from the North. The wind brought ice around them, and except for the feathers they would have perished. As it was, they were almost frozen and sat there through the night with chattering teeth. In the morning Sun called up to them, "Are you dead yet?" They came running down and on the advice of Spider Woman said, "Oh, no, we had a fine place to sleep, except it was too hot. It made us sweat." They pretended to be wiping sweat from their brows. "Now surely you know we are your sons." But Sun said, "Wait a while."

He led them to a place where there was a smooth path, and there were four large hollow spheres of flint. In each of these spheres was a hot fire. Sun bowled one of the spheres along the trail and told one of the Twins to run after it and catch it. He then bowled the other and told the other Twin to run and catch it. Then he bowled the other two spheres at them, crying to them to be sure and stop them. They did. He next told them to pick them up and bring them to him. They were very heavy, but the Twins spurted medicine on them and they became light. They took them up in their hands and brought them to Sun.

Then Sun recognized them as his sons. He cleansed and decorated them, and his wife was no longer angry at them. He sat each of them on a turquoise mound. He showed them beautiful clouds in one room, asking them if they wished to take some of these. The Twins said, "No." He showed them beautiful shells and ornaments of all kinds, and beautiful garments, and all manner of animals. These he offered as gifts to them. But the Twins did not want them. "Well," he said, "you must desire something. Tell me what it is." So they said they wanted weapons to destroy the monsters that ravaged their mother's land. Sun then gave them bow and arrow and resilient lightning.

Meanwhile, the separation had been going on for three years. The woman's gowns had grown ragged and their fields were poorly cultivated. On the fourth year the men again had abundant harvests, but the women obtained little from the fields, and they were hungry and unhappy. On the morning of the fifth Winter solstice ceremony after separation, the woman chief came to the river bank and called across to the men, "I want to tell you something." A youth heard her and told the elder men and one of them went to the river bank and called, "What is it you have to say?" The woman chief was all in rags and looked miserable. She said, "I have been thinking, let all the men and youths assemble on your side and all the women and virgins on this side and let us discuss. This was agreed to and they all assembled. The woman chief spoke first, "We are all in rags, and we have only a few ears of corn left to eat. We have no meat, no copulation, no child-bearing. We are sad." "True," said the chief. The woman chief said, "Let some men come over here." "Let the women come over here," said the chief. The women were all glad of this and ran into the water and swam across. The men received them gladly. The men had built fine houses, and these they gave to the women. They had also woven many fine gowns and girdles, and these they gave to the women also, and there was an abundance of corn, and plenty of elk, deer, bear, and antelope.

At that time, at sunrise the sky was wide. The horizon was far around. But at noon, the sky vibrated. It alternately compressed and distended. The horizon was not so far around as it is in this world. In the daytime, in the Underworld, it was beautiful. There was bubbling water, all around the landscape. But at night the sky contracted and it was disagreeable. There were both sun and moon at that time. Then the bubbling waters increased and encroached upon the dry land and pressed close towards the people. They became sad. The chief thought and said, "Perhaps there is a doorway to this sky."

There were four mountains at the cardinal points. At the mountain at the Northeast lived Spider Woman and the Twins. The Hopi War chief made a war prayer-stick for Spider Woman and a club for the Twins, and prayer-feathers, and sent a youth with these to the mountain. Spider Woman thanked the youth for the prayer-stick and prayer-feathers and asked what he wanted. The

Twins danced with joy over their presents. "What do you wish
for these things?" asked Spider Woman. The youth said, "We
are surrounded by bubbling water, and it is covering all our land.
Where is a good place to go to, the good houses. Perhaps you
know." "Yes," she said, "I know. In the above is a good place;
tell all your people to hurry and come here." The youth returned,
and after the elders assembled and smoked, he told all. Women
prepared food for the journey, and then all the people started, carrying altar slabs on their backs, and went to the mountain. They
all went up the mountain to its peak, and the water followed close
behind them. The water covered everything, but the mountain grew
a little faster than the rise of the water, and after a time the
mountain summit was almost touching the sky. Spider Woman
planted spruce plant and it grew up against the sky, but the sky
was hard and the spruce could not penetrate it. Again Spider
Woman thought, "Perhaps reed will pass through." So she planted
a reed, and it grew four days and reached the sky and found a
small crevice which it penetrated. Badger climbed its stalk and
reached its tip, but he could not get through to see anything, so
he returned saying, "I am very tired. I can see nothing but earth."
The elders thought, "What man knows? Perhaps Locust." So they
asked him, and he said, "Yes, I know." Locust is very brave.
He never winks his eyes. So he climbed the stalk and went through
and reached the tasselled tip of the reed, and looked around, and
there was water everywhere. Locust carried a flute, slung on his
back. He drew it out and began to play on it. At the Northwest
the Yellow Cloud chief appeared. He was angry and darted yellow
lightning which went close past the eyes of Locust. But Locust
never winked, and went on playing his flute. Yellow Cloud said,
"What kind of man have we here? Surely he is brave, surely he
is a man!" Next at the Southwest Blue Cloud chief appeared, and
he was angry too and flung blue lightning at Locust and it passed
through him from side to side. But Locust continued to play as
before, and Blue Cloud said the same about him as had Yellow
Cloud. Then at the Southeast, Red Cloud came up very angry and
darted red lightning which passed through Locust from belly to
back, and he continued playing as if nothing had happened. Red
Cloud expressed his wonder and said what the other Clouds had
said. At the Northeast White Cloud arose and cast white lightning
which passed through Locust from head to tail, and he continued
playing as if nothing had happened to him. The four Cloud chiefs
came close to Locust and talked with him, demanding to know where
he came from. They said, "This is the land of the Clouds. What

are you doing here?   You are a good and brave man.   Perhaps you are an orphan."   "No," said Locust.   "I have many people behind me in the Underworld."   "It is well," said the Cloud chiefs. "You are brave and deathless.   Your heart and those of your people must be good.   Go tell them to come and all this land shall be theirs."   "Thanks," said Locust, and he then returned and told his people.   Then Badger went up and widened the opening so that the people could pass through.   While he was doing this, Locust told of his adventures to the people and said that the place above was just like the place they were then at, all water.   The people were saddened at this, but the chiefs thought, and said, "Well, it is no worse than here and may be better.   Let's go up and see."   The people climbed the reed for eight days, stopping each night at a joint from which a great leaf grew out, and the people slept on it. That is why these leaves are called "sleeps".

When all had emerged, the Twins who each had the resilient lightning shot it in every direction and made canyons through which the water flowed away.   The Twins then made all the rocks of mud and made all the mountains and made everything that is of stone. Later they slew the Giant Eagle and the Giant Elk and other monsters.

2. THE EARTHDIVER

(Western Mono)

In the beginning, Prairie Falcon and Crow were sitting on a log which projected above the waters that covered the world.   They asked Duck what number he had dreamed of, and Duck replied, "Two."   Prairie Falcon assigned him the number three and told him to dive into the water and bring up some sand from the bottom.   Duck dived to get the sand, but before he reached the bottom, the three days he had been allotted expired.   He awoke from his dream, died, and floated to the surface.   Prairie Falcon brought him back to life, however, and asked him what the trouble was. Duck said that he had come out of his dream, died, and then floated to the top.

Prairie Falcon now asked Coot what number he had dreamed of.   Coot replied, "Four."   Then Prairie Falcon assigned him the number two and ordered him to dive for sand.   Before Coot reached the bottom, two days elapsed, and he came out of his dream. He too died, and his body floated to the surface of the waters. Prairie Falcon saw the corpse, recovered it, and brought Coot back to life. He asked Coot what had been the trouble, and Coot replied that he had passed out of his dream.

Then Prairie Falcon asked Grebe what number he had dreamed of. Grebe replied that he had dreamed of five. Prairie Falcon assigned him the number four, and told him that was the number of days he had to bring sand from the bottom of the waters. Grebe was successful   He dived all the way to the bottom of the waters and secured some sand in each hand. As he was returning to the surface, he passed out of his dream, died, and floated to the surface. Prairie Falcon brought him back to life and asked if he had secured any sand. Grebe said that he had, so Prairie Falcon wanted to know what he had done with it. Grebe explained that it had all slipped from his grasp when he died. Prairie Falcon and Crow both laughed at him and said that they didn't believe him. Then they looked at his hands and found sand under the fingernails. They took that sand and threw it in every direction. This is the way in which they made the world.

Nearly all Indian tribes account for the coming of death into the world. Often the story involves a debate in which one character wants people to die and be revived and the other wants dying to be permanent. The second character wins out, much to his regret when one of his loved ones perishes and cannot be brought back to life. The San Luiseño tale that follows is unique to the California area and accounts for the origin of the moon, proper food, certain sacrifices, and certain tabus. It is obviously part of the origin story.

3. OUIOT AND FROG

(San Luiseño)

While they were all living at Temecula, there was a man among them, Ouiot, who was very wise and who knew more than anyone living. He taught the people and watched over them and made provision for their needs. He called them all his children.

It was a custom for all the people to take a bath every morning. Among them was a beautiful woman whom Ouiot had especially admired. She had a beautiful face and long hair that fell down to her feet, completely covering her back. She always went down to the water when no one else was there and would bathe when no one could see her. Ouiot noticed this and made it a point to watch her one day. When she jumped into the water, he saw that her back was hollow and flat like that of a frog, and his admiration turned to disgust.

The woman, Frog, observed Ouiot and read his thoughts. She was filled with anger against him. When she told her people of his feelings towards her, they conspired together saying, "We will kill him." So the four of them, Frog, Earthworm, Gopher, and Water Animal, decided to destroy him by witchcraft. As soon as they had finished their witchcraft, Ouiot fell sick. He tried in vain to ease his pain. He sent north, south, east and west for remedies, but nothing could help him. He grew so much worse that he lay helpless, unable to rise. Frog and her helpers came and jeered at him, and because he lingered so long in his illness, they gave him the name Ouiot. Myola was his real name.

Then a man, named Rattlesnake, arose and said. "What is the matter with all you people? You call yourselves witches, yet you cannot cure our sick brother." So Rattlesnake, who knew everything, searched north, south, east, and west, trying to find some way to help Ouiot, or to learn what was the matter with him. But it was all in vain. After him another man, Horned Toad, equally great, went about searching for a remedy, trying his best, but without success. Next Roadrunner stood up. He examined Ouiot and searched about among the people to see if any of them had caused his illness. But he could discover nothing. Next came Little Bird. He did the same thing. He examined Ouiot and told the people that someone had poisoned him and that he was going to die.

Ouiot was getting worse all the time, and he called his best friend, Kingbird, a great captain and a very good man, and told him that he had been poisoned and named the four who had caused it and told him why they had done it and that he was soon to die. To Kingbird alone he revealed the truth that he would return. "Look towards the east for my coming in the early morning," he said. Thus Kingbird knew the secret. Then he summoned all the rest of the people that he might give them his final commands. When all had gathered together, some of his children raised him in their arms so that he could sit up and address them. The tears began to run down his cheeks. Coyote, Bluefly, and Buzzard crowded about him wanting to eat his body. Coyote began licking his tears. Then Ouiot said that his death might come in the first month or in the second part of the first month. But this time passed and he was still alive. "Perhaps, I shall die next month or in the second part of the next month." This also passed. So he predicted his death in each successive month, only to linger through until the last. In the last month, he died, and death came into the world. No one had died before.

There was a man, Kangaroo-Rat, who made a carrying-net in which to lift Ouiot. They sent to all four points of the compass for wood, the sycamore, black oak, white oak, tule, hemlock, and cedar, in order to build the funeral fire. They got a hollow log, and on the lower half they laid the body. Then they put the other half of the log above it for a lid. After the pile of wood was ready and the fire lighted, the men carried the body in the net and after circling the fire three times laid it on the flames.

Coyote, who wanted to eat the body, was sent away. He ran off but looking back, he saw the smoke of the burning fire rising up to the sky. So he turned and came running back with all his might. They took sticks and tried to drive him away, and they stood in a circle close together about the fire to prevent him from approaching it. But Badger was only a little man, and Coyote ran at him and jumped over his head. He snatched the heart, the only part of the body that was not consumed by the flames, and ran off with it, devouring it.

There was a man among them named Little Squirrel, and when Ouiot was burned he stood up and addressed the people. He called the clouds from the mountains to come, and the clouds and fog from the sea to gather, and to fall in showers upon the earth to blot out all tracks that Ouiot had made when he moved upon the world. He asked that none be left. So the clouds came, and it rained heavily.

Ouiot had told them that in time to come they must have fiestas for the dead and that they must begin to kill and eat for food. Until this time they had never eaten flesh or grains, but had lived on clay. They discussed the matter, questioning who should be killed first. One man after another was chosen, but each refused in turn.

Ouiot had said that Eagle must be killed at the time of every fiesta, and Eagle did not like this. To escape, he went north, south, east and west. But there was death for him everywhere, and he came back and gave himself up. Hummingbird said that he would like to take Eagle's place. He felt that he was a person of importance. But the people said, "No! You are a little man, not fit for that." And they would not let him.

Ouiot had also said they could eat Deer. They talked about killing Deer. "He is a nice-looking man; he would be good for meat." Lion was a strong, powerful man, and he said, "Why do you delay and discuss? This is the way it should be done." So he fell on Deer and killed him, and the others that had been selected to be animals were killed at the same time. They turned into different kinds of animals and different kinds of grain, and all the things we see now in the world.

When they killed Deer, they took the small pointed bones of the leg to use as awls for making baskets. A fine basket was made, and the bones and ashes of Ouiot were placed in it. They buried the basket in the ground. While they were burying it, they sang solemn words with groans and they danced. This was the first time there had been singing or dancing for the dead. Rabbit was the man who sang first, and Crow and Wild Goose danced first.

After the fiesta was over, they had a big meeting at Temecula, where they were still together. They had found out that death had come into the world and they didn't know what to do. They discussed the matter. All those that are now stars went up into the sky at this time, hoping to escape death in this manner. And all things that live in the ground, worms, insects, and burrowing animals, went underground to hide from death. But others decided to stay on earth. They figured that it might be possible to live for a certain number of years and then to go back and be young again. Then they all left Temecula and scattered all over, just as it is today. Now that Ouiot was gone there was no use staying in their first home. They no longer had a guide and teacher there.

No one knew that Ouiot was to come back, except Kingbird. Early in the morning, he would go to the housetop and call out, "Ouiot is coming back." "What does he say?" the people wondered. They did not understand, until Ouiot rose as the moon in the east. They saw the moon rise, and they knew it was Ouiot. It was the first time the moon had ever come, but it has risen ever since.

Theft stories are known to tribes all across the Continent. Fire, daylight, the sun, the moon, water, game, all have to be released from the control of some figure who has withheld them from mankind. The tales of the theft of fire and of the theft of light are by far the most widespread, the latter being exceptionally common to the Pacific Coastal tribes. The two tests that follow represent the two most popular forms the story takes. In both cases, as was discussed in the Introduction, the figure who controls the element man needs is powerless to prevent the theft, although he is noticeably suspicious his treasure is to be taken.

4. THEFT OF FIRE

(Southern Paiute)

Many people lived around here, but they had no fire. They had only a heated stone. The people were always hunting rabbits. Coyote was on the edge of the hunter's line. He saw the ashes of a fire coming from somewhere and dropping to the ground. He yelled to the others, and they came, gathering round in a circle to watch. While watching they said, "Some one shall go up into the air and find out where it comes from." Eagle said, "Let me try first to see whether I can get high enough to see." He went up and out of sight, but returned without having seen it. Chickenhawk set out next, but he did not go out of sight. Woodpecker also did not get very far; they were able to see him. All the birds tried, but none could go far enough. Only Fish was left. They said, "You have no wings, how are you going to go up?" --- "Let me try for fun whether or not I can fly." He started up. He went out of sight, and when he returned he said, "Not very far from here are flames of fire, near a snow-topped mountain peak." Coyote said, "Let's go and get it; that's not far." All started, Coyote leading, and Woodpecker, Chickenhawk, Blue Jay, Roadrunner, Jackrabbit, and others following. They went toward the place where fire had been seen and made firedrills to take along so as to deceive the fireowners and prevent them from guessing what their visitors were seeking.

When they arrived Coyote made a speech: "We have merely come for fun, to gamble and play with you." The hosts gave all the animals the kind of food they were used to eat, to each bird a different kind of seed, to Crested Jay good hard pinenuts. To Coyote they gave cedar berries. After they had eaten, they began to play. They made three piles of dirt and hid something in one of the piles. If the guesser hit the right pile with a stone, he won the game. All night they played. The hosts said, "These people have not come to gamble; they have come to steal our fire." Coyote replied, "No, we have fire ourselves," and showed them their firedrills. Towards morning Coyote had some cedarbark tied to his hair and let it stick out. When he tied it on, all were watching him circling round. "We know what they have come for," they said. At daylight Coyote bent over the fire, then the bark caught fire, and he jumped away over the crowd and ran off followed by his people. Before very long Crested Jay was caught and killed by the pursuers. One after another carried the fire. When they reached the Colorado River, all the rest were tired and Roadrunner said, "Let me carry the fire." He put it on each side of his head. Then he tore his feet in different ways so that they could not see the direction he had taken and made lots of sand. The pursuers tracked him, some backwards, others forwards, and did not know which way to go. He arrived in the Shivwits country. They tracked him. He built a big fire on the top of a mountain. Looking up, the pursuers saw the big fire. Then they went back.

In the evening Coyote's people saw clouds. It was going to rain. Coyote carried together plenty of wood. His people went into a cave for shelter. After dark it rained. They built a big fire, but the water put it out. They saved one charcoal, and in the morning they told Jackrabbit to hold it. He took it into the rain. Coyote told him not to let it go out, or he would shoot him. But Jackrabbit kept it under his tail and saved it. The rain ceased, then Jackrabbit brought the coal back, and it was still alive. Everything was wet, however, and they could not find any tinder. Rat said, "I have a dry nest to make fire with." He gave it to them and they had a big fire. Coyote said to his followers, "Let's give heat and fire to all the trees and shrubs and to all the rocks." So he gave fire to everyone of them so they should burn thereafter. Then he dried his bow and arrows, and called Rat to come out by imitating his noise. When Rat came, Coyote shot and killed him, and roasted him in the fire. After that he killed Jackrabbit, skinned him, and made a blanket of the skin. He killed nearly all of those with him and ate them. "Hereafter, people shall do thus."

5. THEFT OF LIGHT

(Tahltan)

At this time there was no daylight, or sun, moon, or stars. Raven went to a village and asked the people if they could see anything. They said, "No, but one man has daylight, which he keeps in a box in his house. When he takes off the lid, there is a bright light in his house." The people could not work much, for it was night continually. Raven found out where Daylight-Man lived and went to his house. The man also had control of the sun, moon, and stars. Raven went into the house and came out again. He planned what to do to get daylight for himself and the people.

Daylight-Man had many slaves, and a daughter who had been a woman for three years. However, she was still undergoing the ceremonies girls undergo at puberty. She lived apart in the corner of the house, in a room of her own, and was closely watched. She drank out of a white bucket every day, and she always examined the water before drinking to see if there was anything in it. Slaves always brought the water to her. Raven changed himself into a cedar leaf in the bucket of water the slave was bringing. The girl noticed it before drinking and threw it out. Raven assumed his natural form again. The next day he transformed himself into a very small cedar leaf and hid in the water. The girl looked in the water, and seeing nothing she drank it all and thus swallowed Raven. The following month she did not menstruate. After three months she began to swell. Her mother noticed this and asked her if she was still not menstruating. She said she had not menstruated for three months. Her mother said, "You are pregnant; you have been with a man." Her parents questioned her, but she denied that a man had been with her. They did not see how she could have been made pregnant, as she had been so closely watched. After nine months she produced a son. The parents said they would rear the boy and acknowledge him as their grandson, even if he had no father. They said, if she told who the father of the child was, they would agree that he marry their daughter. They would treat their son-in-law well, and all would be well. But she continued to say that she had seen no man.

The boy grew very fast and soon was able to walk and talk. His grandfather loved him dearly. One day he cried very much and wanted to be allowed to play with the moon. His grandfather ordered the moon to be taken and given to him. The boy was pleased and played with the moon until he was tired. Then, they hung it up again. After a while he got tired of the moon and cried much, saying that he wanted the sun. It was given to him and he played with it till he was tired; then he gave it back, and the people hung it up again. After a while he became tired of the sun and called for the Big Dipper. They allowed him to play with these things whenever he wanted. After a long time, when he felt strong, he cried for the daylight. His grandfather was afraid to give it to him, because it shed so much light. Also, whenever it was lifted up, the sun, moon, and stars, and everything worked in unison with it. It was their chief. At last, however, the boy was allowed to play with daylight. But his grandfather was uneasy when he did. When the boy lifted up daylight, much light would come, and the higher he held it the brighter became the daylight. On occasions when the boy held the daylight high, the old man would say, "Eh, eh!" as if he were hurt or extremely anxious. The boy balanced daylight on his hands to get used to carrying it.

At last, he felt strong enough for the feat he intended to perform. He put two of the toys in each hand and balanced them. He felt he could carry them easily. Then, at a moment when the people weren't watching, he flew out of the smoke-hole with them. He threw daylight away, saying, "From now on there shall be daylight, and people will be able to see and work and travel. After dawn the sun will rise, and when it sets night will come. People will then rest and sleep, for it will not be easy to work and travel. Then the Dipper and the moon will go out and give light. These things shall never again belong to one man, nor be locked up in one place. They shall be for all people". He threw daylight to the north, the sun to the east, the moon to the west, and the Dipper to the south. Since then, people and game rise with daylight and go to sleep with nightfall.

Tales 6 through 11 represent typical Indian attempts to explain natural phenomena. Peoples all over the world have or have had such stories, but there are few accounts anywhere in world literature that match these half-dozen for beauty and imagination.

The Iroquois tale of the origin of the winds is an integral part of the origin myth, The Woman Who Fell from the Sky, and was utilized in a much milder form by Longfellow in his poem, Hiawatha. Longfellow, following the lead of an early scholar, Henry Rowe Schoolcraft, confused Hiawatha, who was actually an Iroquoian statesman, with the Ojibwa culture hero, Nanibozho or Naniboju. Thus, even though the hero of the poem has an Iroquoian name, he is made to act out Ojibwa legends. Oddly, however, Ojibwa and Iroquois mythology share the portion of the tale printed here.

The Shasta myth, which involves the regulation of the sun, might well be compared with Tale 26, The Sun-Snare, which concerns the World Fire --- a calamity not unlike the Biblical flood story. Tales 8 and 9 also complement each other, in that they both account for the origin of the Seven Stars. The Onandaga myth makes the origin of the stars the central theme of the tale. Tale 9 is somewhat more typical of the North American Indian in that the origin of the Pleiades is clearly incidental to the main plot of animal marriage.

Animal marriages are common to the tales of most primitive people. For the Indian, with his concept that at one time animals were men, such stories were easy to accept, and girls marry everything from snakes to bears to birds in his tales. Stories in which a girl marries a dog were known widely on the Western Plains, among the North Pacific groups, and to the Eskimo.

6. HOW THE FOUR WINDS WERE CREATED

(Ojibwa)

This happened a long time ago, long ago when all things were young. At that time there lived an old woman and a girl in a certain place. The girl was unmarried and childless. Her mother was very careful about her. At the time of the birth of the girl, she had a premonition misfortune would come to the child. She was told in a dream that the child should never at any time face the place of the going down of the sun. When she went out to urinate, even after she became a woman she had to be careful about this thing. If she should not, some great trouble would certainly happen to her. The mother was very careful with her daughter through childhood. However, people can't always be children. Reaching girlhood and womanhood, the daughter of the now old woman, had to care for herself. But the mother was very careful to explain to her that things even worse than the sky falling on her would result, if she should face the setting sun. The girl heeded the warning and was careful about this thing.

But one day she went into the woods by herself. It was a foggy day. As she was wandering about, she lost her way. While searching about to find a way home, she needed to urinate. Unfortunately, she faced the wrong direction. She felt queer at once. At the same moment a great whirlwind came and blew her clothing all up over her head, leaving her nude to her waist. After the wind went down, and the girl righted her clothes, she searched about the woods and at last found her way home. On arriving home, she told her mother about her experience and her peculiar feelings.

On hearing her daughter's words, the mother who was sitting with her back to the door-entrance faced about, and she at once decided that this was the beginning of great misfortune for her family. The girl stood before her trembling from head to foot and white as the whitest snow. When the mother recovered enough to speak, she asked the girl: "Have you gone and faced in the wrong direction?"

"Yes, mother," said the girl, sinking to the floor and burying her face in her hands. "Yes, mother, but I did not do it on purpose. But I know that I must suffer. Even now, I know that I am pregnant."

Time passed and the girl was in great trouble. It was evident that more than one child was in her womb. There was great struggling there, with pain to the mother. The children were fighting with each other, for supremacy, for possession of the powers that be. They could even be heard talking as they fought. One said, "I am first." Then another and another said the same. Then there would be a great fight. The poor mother! Finally, one day the time to give birth had about arrived. There was a greater struggle in the womb than ever before, and greater fighting. Suddenly, the mother was torn to bits by the fighters and scattered in little pieces to the ends of all space. Even the mother of the girl found herself blown many miles.

The children that were born were the four winds, of which Manabozho is the chief. Even in the womb these four winds could not get along with each other. When still young, they separated. They divided the space of the earth and sky equally between them. Manabozho took the space toward the coming of the sun. He is now the strong east wind.

7. COYOTE ARRANGES THE SEASONS OF THE YEAR

(Shasta)

After Coyote had come back from across the ocean, he stayed with his wife one year in the Joshua country and built himself a sweathouse there. He was in the habit of leaving his wife frequently for the purpose of hunting and fishing. A little ways up the river he had a house for drying salmon. One day he went to the drying-house and stayed there a month. Then he went back to his wife, carrying all the dried salmon in a canoe. After his return he went out on the beach at low tide, where he found plenty of eels with red backs. This surprised him, and he concluded that spring must have come. It seemed to him that he must have missed a good many months. He could not understand this, so he decided to go upstream to a prairie and view the country from there. Arriving at that place, he saw that all the flowers were dry. This convinced him that he had missed all the winter months. So he went back and said to his wife, "My wife, everything upstream is dry. It will be midsummer soon." But the woman laughed at him. Then Coyote told her to throw all the old salmon into the river, as he did not want to mix old salmon with fresh eels. The woman refused to do so, and they quarrelled over it for a long time. She suspected that some one had been playing a trick on her husband, so she decided to hide all the food she could find and store it away. She did not believe that fall was coming. Coyote thought that his wife had thrown all the old salmon away, as he had told her to do, and went out to gather fresh eels.

But he did not see a single eel. He thought, "Well, the eels will come tonight." He went back to his wife and told her about his failure. She paid no attention to him, but kept on eating the salmon she had saved up. At night Coyote went out again. He fished a whole night, but did not catch a single eel. In the morning he was very hungry, so he went down to the beach in the hope of finding something to eat. Again he was disappointed. Nothing had drifted ashore. In the evening he went out fishing again. He was very hungry by this time and suspected that either the Sun or the Moon had fooled him. For nearly a month he had nothing to eat. He was so weak that he could hardly walk. And all this time his wife was eating the meat she had stored away without his knowledge.

One day Coyote called all the animals and birds together, told them how the Sun had fooled him and asked them to help him kill the Sun. Coyote was given food which made him feel stronger. Then they started out in quest of the place where the Sun usually comes out. They built a fort there, covered it with tips, and made a small hole through which to watch the Sun. Coyote had also made a knife and was ready to catch the Sun as soon as he should come up and to kill him. He watched. Towards daylight the Sun appeared way off. So Coyote told his companions to take a good rest that day, after which they would go to the place from where the Sun had emerged. They started again. Coyote spoke to the land, and the distance shortened. Soon they came to a new place and made themselves ready. Again the Sun came out, but he was so far that Coyote could hardly see him. Again he told his friends to rest. In the evening they started out once more. Again Coyote shortened the distance by a mere wish. They came to the new place, but the Sun was still far off. The same thing happened twenty times. At last, they came to a high mountain, which the Sun could hardly make. Then Coyote was glad and said, "Now we shall surely catch him." So the next night they went to a new place, Coyote shortening the distance as before. Quite a number of his companions were already worn out with hunger and fatigue and had dropped out. The new place they came to had high mountains on both sides. They made a high wall between these and felt sure that they should catch the Sun in this place. At night they got ready. Daylight began to appear, and Coyote warned his friends to beware of any tricks that the Sun might play on them. "He may come out from the ground with his eyes shut," he said, "so that you won't see him until he opens his eyes on top of the mountain, and then he will be out of reach." At last the Sun appeared at the foot of the slope on the other side of the mountain. He looked very large and was quite a distance away. So Coyote told his friends to rest that day. He felt sure that they would catch the Sun at night. After sundown they started out and came to a large body of water. Coyote held a council with his people and asked them to look for a place to cross the ocean. Half he sent north, while the other half was to go south. He thought perhaps the Sun might have his house in the water. Soon they saw lots of reeds. Coyote's friends became discouraged and wanted to go home, but he encouraged them, saying that he had been there before. They were very tired and hungry. So Coyote advised them to eat some roots. These kept them alive, and from that time on people learned the use of roots as medicine. From the shore they saw a large fog on the other side of the ocean, which disappeared as soon as the Sun came out. Then they were sure that they were near the Sun's lodge. At noon the Sun came up high above them; he was still very far. They did not know how to cross the ocean. So Coyote called on the water-people to help him. Ten times he called, but no one came. Then he nearly lost his courage. He and his companions were almost starved to death.

Finally Coyote said to one of his companions, "Strike me over the head twice! Something may happen." His companion refused, fearing he might kill him. Coyote insisted, and told his friends that if he dropped senseless, they should let him lie until some one came, and then they should push him. So Coyote sat down, closed his eyes, and his companion hit him on the side of the head with a stick. A cracking sound was heard. Twice Coyote was hit before he fell to the ground lifeless. Then the people began to wonder how they should get home without Coyote; he had taken them so far away from home. Night came, and they heard the sound of mice squeaking around them in a circle. At first they did not wake Coyote. Three times the mice went around them before the people thought of waking Coyote. At first they called his name, then they shook him. At last Coyote stretched himself and said, "Oh, I am sleepy!" His friends yelled at him, "Some one has come!" Then Coyote opened his eyes, squeezed his head on all sides, and it got well again. Soon the mice began to squeak, and Coyote called to them, "My grandsons, come to me!" Then two mice appeared. They had no tails; their ears were small; and their hair was very short. Coyote told them that he was their uncle and that their father was a great friend of his. The mice listened in silence. Then Coyote asked them to tell him where the house of the Sun was. The bigger mouse said, "If you give us what we want, we will tell you where the Sun's house is located."

--- "What do you want?" asked Coyote, "dentalia shells?" The mouse shook its head. Coyote offered them all kinds of valuables, but the mice did not want them. The night was passing fast, and Coyote was in a hurry, so he took a salmon-net and made two tails of it. To one mouse he gave the long tail, while the other received a short tail. He also gave them ears and hair of different colors. At last he asked them if they were satisfied, and the Mice replied, "Yes." Then Coyote took some fat and rubbed it on their noses and told them that thereafter they would smell grease, even from a long distance; and this is the reason why all mice today like grease and why they get into salmon-nets and tear them whenever they are hung up. They do this because their tails were made of salmon-nets.

Then Coyote asked the mice, "How do you cross the ocean?" The mice told him that they had a trail under water. He also inquired about the house of Sun and Moon and learned that there were one hundred Suns and Moons and that the Suns and the Moons were the same people. One person would appear as a Sun one day. Upon his return, another man would go out as Moon. Then he would come back and go to sleep, and another person would go out as Sun ---and so on. Coyote wanted to know if there were any sweathouses there. "Only one," said the mice, "and it is very hot." They also told him that whenever a Sun wanted to enter the sweathouse, he would first thrust his foot in, and then jump out quickly. Then he would go in again and jump out. He would do this five times before remaining in the sweathouse for good. "Then," the mice said, "you can catch him." Coyote also found out that the Moon's country was dry, had no water, and that it was always hot and light there. He also asked the Mice, "Which Sun fooled me last fall?" The mice answered, "There were two of them. Their names are Windy Moon and Bad Sun. They are very bad and make all sorts of trouble. The others are good." Coyote wanted to know how big they were. "Very big," the mice said, "and very dangerous." Then Coyote told the mice that he and his companions would rest a whole day and would make the attack on the Suns and the Moons the next night. He asked the mice to go home and to gnaw through all the bow-strings in the houses of the Suns and Moons. At last he asked them, "Did you say these houses were under water?" --- "No!" replied the mice, "they are on land." Coyote suspected the mice of lying, but decided to take chances. Then he asked, "How far is it from here?" --- "A long ways off!" The mice were ready to start at noon. Coyote wanted to know how long the Suns stayed in the sweathouse and if they had any dogs. "There are

no dogs," the Mice said. Then they continued, "None of the Suns
urinates very much, excepting the two we mentioned before. These
two leave the house often and urinate for a long time. Whenever
they do so, it rains and storms very hard. Watch these two carefully, for they are the ones who played the trick on you." Just
before the mice departed, they agreed to warn Coyote of any lurk-
ing danger by squeaking. They opened the door and disappeared.

   Coyote called his people together and held a council. It was
decided to eat the Suns and Moons as soon as they should be killed,
for in that country there was no place to bury them. Then he
ordered the ocean to become small and dry and started out with
his people. Soon the light began to grow very bright; they were
approaching the home of the Suns and Moons. The sand was ex-
ceedingly hot. They came to the sweathouse. Coyote hid his
companions in it, while he himself knelt down inside near the door,
where he could catch anyone who went in, kill him, and throw him
to his friends. Soon he heard the mice squeaking and whispered,
"My children, I am here!" The mice told him that all the Suns
and Moons were in the house, so Coyote caused a heavy fog to
spread over the place. The mice said, "The people saw our new
tails and furs and wondered what it meant. They are surprised
and suspect that Coyote has done this and is watching them. We
have eaten up all the bows and strings in the houses." Coyote was
glad. Then one mouse went back into the house, while the other
remained outside to give warning. Soon everything became quiet.
After a little while Coyote heard the slow, heavy footsteps of an
approaching Sun and saw a bright light, accompanied by a faint
hissing sound. Then a foot was thrust into the sweathouse and
quickly withdrawn. Four times this process was repeated. After
the fifth time a Sun put the whole body in, whereupon Coyote killed
him, threw him to his people, who ate him up at once. And from
that time on the birds and Coyote have been in the habit of eating
dead corpses.

   In this manner he killed fifty persons, leaving fifty Suns to
shine each week of the year. After the first twenty-five had been
killed, Coyote's people became full and could not eat anymore. So
the place began to smell of blood, and the other Suns became
suspicious. At last Windy Moon started for the sweathouse. He
approached, causing a great noise and wind. Coyote trembled with
excitement. Windy Moon urinated for a long time. As he came
nearer to the sweathouse, he wondered why it was dark inside.
He put his foot in, then withdrew it quickly. Coyote began to waver;
he thought that perhaps he had killed enough Suns and Moons. At

last Windy Moon came in. Coyote stabbed him, but only scratched his rump. The wounded Sun rushed into the house and gave the alarm. Coyote quickly gathered his people and told them to disperse. Then he produced a heavy fog, so that he could not be seen. The Moons woke up and seized their bows and arrows, but all were gnawed through. Thus Coyote and his friends escaped. The mice also went home on their trail. They met at their first meeting-place, and Coyote danced the death-dance. Since then people have always danced the murder-dance. The wounded Moon had a very bad night; he was quite sick.

At noon Coyote looked up at the sky and said, "Suns, if you ever fool me again, I will return and kill you all!" The Suns did not answer. Then Coyote settled the length of the year and divided it into twelve periods. The Suns have never dared to disobey him.

8. THE ORIGIN OF THE PLEIADES

(Onondaga)

Once a party of Indians went through the woods toward a hunting-ground which they had known for a long time. They travelled several days through very wild country, going slowly and camping on the way. At last they reached The Beautiful Lake of gray rocks and the great forest trees. Fish swarmed in the waters, and deer came down from the hills to drink. On the hills and in the valleys were huge beech and chestnut trees, where there were squirrels and bears.

The chief of the party was Tracks-in-the-Water, and he halted the group on the shore of the lake to give thanks to the Great Spirit for the safe arrival at the hunting-grounds. "Here we will build our lodges for the winter and may the Great Spirit send us plenty of game and health and peace."

Autumn passed on. The lodges were built and hunting went well. The children began to dance to amuse themselves. They were getting lonesome, having nothing to do, so they went to a quiet spot by the lake to dance. They had done this a long time, when one day a very old man came to them. They had never seen anyone like him before. He was dressed in white feathers and his white hair shone like silver. He spoke to them, telling them they must stop dancing, or evil would happen to them. The children did not pay any attention to him. Day after day they danced. Again and again he appeared, repeating his warning.

One of the children suggested a feast the next time they met to dance. When they returned home, they all asked their parents for food. "You will waste and spoil good food," said one. "You can eat at home as you should," said another. So they got nothing. But they met again and danced anyway. They would have liked to have had something to eat after each dance. Their stomachs were empty.

One day, as they danced, they found themselves rising little by little into the air. Their heads were light from hunger. They didn't know how all this happened. One said, "Don't look back, for something strange is happening." A woman, who saw them, called them back, but with no effect, for they continued to rise slowly above the earth. She ran to the camp, and everyone rushed out with all kinds of food. But the children did not return, even though their parents cried after them.

One, who did look back, became a falling star. The others reached the sky. They are the Pleiades. Every falling star brings the story to mind, but the seven stars shine on --- a band of dancing children.

9. THE GIRL WHO MARRIED A DOG

(Cheyenne)

A chief had a fine looking daughter. She had a great many admirers. At night she was visited by a young man, but she did not know who he was. She worried about this and determined to discover him. She put red paint near her bed. When he crawled on her bed, she put her hand into the paint. When they embraced, she left red marks on his back.

The next day she told her father to call all the young men to a dance in front of his tent. They all came, and the whole village turned out to see them. She watched all that came, looking for the red marks she had made. As she turned about, she caught sight of one of her father's dogs with red marks on his back. This made her so unhappy and she went straight into her tent. This broke up the dance.

The next day she went into the woods near the camp, taking the dog on a string. She hit him. He finally broke loose. She was very unhappy, and several months later she bore seven pups. She told her mother to kill them, but her mother was kind toward them and made a little shelter for them. They began to grow, and sometimes at night the old dog came to them. After a time, the woman began to take an interest in them and sometimes played with them. When they were big enough to run, the old dog came and took them away.

When the woman went to see them in the morning, they were gone. She saw the large dog's tracks, and several little ones, and followed them at a distance. She was sad and cried. She returned to her mother and said, "Mother, make me seven pairs of moccasins. I am going to follow the little ones, searching for them." Her mother made seven pairs of moccasins, and the woman started out, tracking them all the way. Finally, in the distance, she saw a tent. The youngest one came to her and said, "Mother, father wants you to go back. We are going home. You cannot come." She said, "No! Wherever you go, I go." She took the little one and carried him to the tent. She entered and saw a young man, who took no notice of her. He gave her a little meat and drink, which did not grow less no matter how much she ate. She tied the little pup to her belt with a string. Next morning, she was left alone and the tent had vanished. She followed the tracks and again came upon them. Four times this happened in the same way. But the fourth time the tracks stopped.

She looked up into the sky. There she saw her seven pups. They had become seven stars, the Pleiades.

10. THE DEER AND THE RAINBOW

(Wyandot)

The animals were greatly distressed and much offended by the works of the Twin-Made-of-Fire. They saw how fortunate Little Turtle was. She spent most of her time keeping the sky. She always came to attend the Great Council, in the Black Cloud, where the springs, ponds, streams, and lakes were.

One day Deer said to Rainbow, "Carry me up to the sky. I must see Little Turtle." Rainbow did not want to do this for Deer at that time, but wanted to consult the Thunder about the matter and so replied, "Come to me in the winter, when I rest on the mountain by the lake. Then I will take you up to the house of Little Turtle."

Deer looked and waited all winter for Rainbow, but Rainbow did not come. When Rainbow came in the summer, Deer said, "I waited all winter for you on the mountain by the lake; you didn't come. Why did you deceive me?" Then Rainbow said, "When you see me in the fog over the lake, come to me; then you can go up. I will carry you up to the house of Little Turtle in the sky."

One day the fog rolled in, in heavy banks and thick masses over the lake. Deer stood on the hill by the lake, waiting and looking for Rainbow. When Rainbow threw a beautiful arch from the lake to the hill, a white and shining light flashed and shone around Deer. A straight path of all colors lay before Deer. It led through a strange forest. Rainbow said, "Follow the beautiful path through the strange woods."

This Deer did. The beautiful way led to the house of Little Turtle in the sky, and Deer went about the sky everywhere. When the Great Council met, Bear said, "Where is Deer? Deer is not yet come to the Council." Then Hawk flew all about to look for Deer, but Hawk could not find Deer in the air. Then Wolf looked in all the woods, but Deer could not be found in the woods anywhere. When Little Turtle came in the Black Cloud, in which were the streams, the lakes, and the ponds, Bear said, "The deer is not yet come to the Council. Where is Deer? There can be no Council without Deer." Little Turtle replied, "Deer is in the sky. Rainbow made a beautiful pathway of all her colors for Deer to come up by."

The Council looked up to the sky and saw Deer running about there. Then Little Turtle showed the Council the beautiful pathway made for Deer. All the animals except Mud Turtle went along the beautiful way which led them up into the sky. There they remain to this day. They may be seen flying or running about the sky.

11. THE FROGS IN THE MOON

(Lillooet)

The three Frog sisters had a house in the swamp. They lived there together. Not very far away a number of people lived in another house. Among them were Snake and Beaver, who were friends. They were handsome men and wanted to marry the Frog girls.

One night Snake went to Frog's house. The girls were in bed. He crawled in with one of them and put his hand on her face. She awoke and asked him who he was. He said he was Snake. When she learned this, she said she wouldn't marry him and told him to leave at once. She called him bad names like "slimy-fellow", "small eyes", and so forth. Snake returned and told Beaver of his failure.

The next night Beaver went to Frog's house. He also crawled in bed with one of the girls and put his hand on her face. She awoke, but when she found out who he was, she told him to get out. She called him names like "short legs", "big belly", "big butt", and so forth. Beaver felt hurt, and going home began to cry. His father asked him what the matter was, and Beaver told him. The father said, "That's nothing. Don't cry. It will rain too much if you do." But Beaver said, "I will to cry."

As Beaver continued to cry, much rain fell. Soon the swamp where the Frogs lived was flooded. Their house was under the water which covered the tops of the tall swamp-grass. The Frogs got cold and went to Beaver's house. They said to Beaver's father, "We wish to marry your sons." But Old Beaver said, "No! you called us bad names."

The water was now running in a regular stream. The Frogs swam away down the stream until they reached a whirlpool. The whirlpool sucked them in, and they descended to the house of the Moon. The Moon invited them to warm themselves at the fire. But they said, "No, we don't want to sit by the fire. We want to sit there." They pointed at him. --- He said, "Here?", pointing at his feet. They said "No, not there." Then he pointed at one part of his body after another. They didn't like any of the places, until he reached his brow. When he said, "Will you sit here?" and pointed to his brow, they all cried out "Yes!" and jumped on his face. This spoiled his looks. The Frog sisters can be seen on the Moon's face even today.

That the present order be as it is now, it was necessary that the many monsters who were supposed to have once roamed the earth be destroyed. Nowhere in literature does one find such a spectacular group of cannibalistic creatures as those that frequent the North American Indian myths. Men who slap their victims to death with their penises, women with toothed vaginas or with sharp elbows, cruel Suns, skeletons that feed on human flesh, giant elks and beavers, even impervious men made of flint or obsidian go their terrifying way through story after story. The task of slaying these orges falls to a series of heroes, many of whom are born miraculously from splinter wounds, tears, afterbirth, blood, and what-have-you. These heroes may be anxious to marry a girl whose cruel father wishes to test them, they may simply go out hunting and be accosted, they may look for trouble, or they may be a culture hero who must put life in order. Sometimes they go alone, sometimes they have twin brothers to aid them. Whatever the arrangement, they succeed, leaving the world a better place than it was, just as their counterparts in the European fairy-tale do. In fact, so similar are these ogre tales to many the Europeans brought over that the Indian learned and pre-served a host of märchen.

The four examples that follow, in addition to Tales 29 and 30, are quite typical of the native Indian form. Tale 12 is one of the most popular of the Plains myths, where it usually is called <u>Thrown Away and Lodge Boy</u>. The bright, shining object that the hero shoots at the end of Tale 13 is of course Loon-Woman's heart.

12. AFTERBIRTH BOY AND LODGE BOY

(Wichita)

There was once a village where there were two chiefs. The village was divided by a street, so that each chief had his part of the village. Each chief had a child. The child of the chief living in the west village was a boy; the child of the chief living in the east village was a girl. The boy and the girl remained single and were not acquainted with one another. In these times, children of prominent families were shown the same respect as was shown their parents. They were protected from danger. The chief's son had a sort of scaffolding fixed up for his bed, which was so high he had to use a ladder to get into it.

Once upon a time the young man set out to visit the young woman. He wanted to find out what sort of a looking woman she was. At the very same time, the girl set out to visit the young man, to see what sort of looking man he was. They both came into the street-like place, and when they saw each other the girl asked the young man where he was going. The young man replied that he was going to see the chief's daughter, and he asked her where she was going. She replied that she was going to see the chief's son. The young man said that he was the chief's son, and the girl said that she was the chief's daughter. They couldn't decied whether to go to the man's home or the girl's home. Finally they decided to go to the young man's home. The next morning the young man's people wondered why he was not up as early as usual. It was the custom of all the family to rise early and sit up late, for the people of the village came around to the chief's place at all times. They usually woke the young man by tapping on the ladder, so they tapped on the ladder to have him come down. When they could not arouse the young man, they sent the old mother up to awake him. When she got there, she found her son sleeping with another person. She came down and told the others about it. She was sent back to ask them to come down from the bed and have breakfast. When they came down, it was learned that the young man's companion was the other chief's daughter.

Meanwhile the other chief wondered why his daughter did not rise as early as usual. She usually rose early and did work inside the lodge. In the village the girl was from, there lived the Coyote. Since the girl was not to be found, the chief called the men and sent them in search of his daughter. The Coyote went all through his own side of the village, and then went to the other chief's side. There he found the girl living with the chief's son. He went back to the girl's father and told where he had found her. After she was found, the chief was angry and sent word that she was never to come back to her home. And the young man's father did not like the way his son had acted.

The time came when the young man decided to leave the village. He told his wife to get what she wanted to take along for the journey. They started at midnight and went towards the south. They went a long way and then stopped for rest and fell asleep. On the next day they continued their journey in search of a new home. They travelled for three days; then they found a good place where there was timber and water. They made their home there. The man went out daily to hunt, so that they might have all the meat they wanted. The woman fixed up a home, building a grass lodge, and there they stayed for a long while. One time, when the man was about to go out hunting, he cut a stick and put some meat on it and set it by the fire to cook. He told his wife the meat was for someone who would come to visit the place, and that she must not look at him. When she should hear him talking, she should get up in bed and cover her head with a robe. The man left to go hunting that day, and the woman stayed and remembered what she had been told.

After her husband had gone, the woman heard someone talking, saying that he was coming to get something to eat. When she heard him, she went to her bed and covered her head. The visitor came in, took down the meat that the woman's husband had placed by the fire, and ate it. Before leaving, he said, "I have eaten the meat and will go back home." When the visitor had gone, the woman got up again, for she had her work to do. It was late in the evening when her husband returned from his hunting-trip. Every time he went hunting he put the meat up before leaving, and when the visitor came the wife would get into her bed so as not to see who he was. Every time he came in and ate she would listen, and it would sound like two persons eating together.

One morning after her husband had left, the woman made a hole in her robe and took a piece of straw that had a hole in it. When the visitor came, she got into her bed and put the robe over her, with the hole over her eye and the straw clutched in her hand. As soon as the visitor came in, he began to eat. After he was finished eating and was starting out, the woman quickly placed the straw in the hole in the robe, looked through it, and saw the person. She saw that he had two faces, one face on the front and one on the back of his head. When she looked at him he turned back, telling the woman that she had disobeyed her husband's orders and that she would be killed.   Then Double-Faced Man took hold of the woman and cut her open.   She was pregnant, so when Double-Faced Man cut her open, he took out a young child which he wrapped in some pieces of robe and put on the back of some timber in the grass lodge.   He then covered the woman again with her robe.   He took the afterbirth and threw it in the water.

When the husband returned, he found that his wife was dead. He was there alone, so he spoke out, saying, "Now you have done wrong, disobeying my orders.   I told you not to run any risk, but you just had to see what sort of person it was who came here. Now he has killed you."   The man took his wife's body to the south, laid her on the ground, and covered her with buffalo robes.   When he came back, he heard a baby crying.   He looked around inside and outside the lodge, but he could not find the baby.   He finally heard the child crying again and the sound came from behind one of the lodge poles.   He looked there and found the child.   He cooked some rare meat and had the child suck the juices.   In this way the man nourished his child.   He stayed with it most of the time and when hunting he carried it on his back.   Whenever he killed any game, he would not hunt any more until all the meat was gone. The child was a boy, and it wasn't very long before he began to walk, though his father would still take him on his back when he went hunting.   When the child was old enough, the father made him a bow and arrows and left him at home when he went hunting.

One day when the boy had been left, he heard someone saying, "My brother, come out and let's have an arrow game."   When he turned around he saw a boy about his own age standing at the entrance of the grass lodge.   The little boy ran out to see the visitor, who said that he was his brother.   They fixed up a place and had a game of arrows.   When Double-Faced man had killed the woman, he had taken a stick that she had used for a poker and stuck it into the afterbirth and thrown it in the water.   This stick was still fastened in the visitor.   The boy wondered what this stick was there for.   They began to play.   The visiting boy promised not to tell their father about winning the arrows, and the other boy promised not to tell that he had had company.   When the visiting boy left, he went toward the river and jumped into the water.

When the father came home he asked his boy what had become of his arrows.   The boy replied that he had lost all his arrows shooting at birds.   His father tried to get him to go where he had been shooting to see if he could find the arrows, but the boy said he could not find the arrows.   Next day the father made other arrows for the boy and went out hunting again. As soon as the father left, the visiting boy came, calling his brother to come out and have another game. They played all day, until the visiting boy won all the arrows. Then he left, going toward the river. When the man came back from his hunting trip, he found the boy with no arrows and asked him what had become of them. The boy said that he had lost his arrows by shooting at birds. The father asked him to go out and look around for the arrows, but the boy refused and said that the arrows could not be found. Again the father made more arrows for his boy.

After a long time the boy told his father of his brother's visits. The father decided to capture the visiting boy one day, so he postponed his hunting trip till another time. About the time the visiting boy usually made his appearance, the father hid himself and turned himself into a piece of stick that they used for a poker. The father told his son to invite his brother to come in and to have something to eat before playing. As soon as the visiting boy came and called his brother, his brother invited him to come in. But he refused, because he was afraid that the old man might be inside. He looked all around, and when he saw the poker he knew at once that it was the old man, and he went off. The father stayed still all that day, intending to capture the boy. On the next day, he again postponed his trip and instructed his boy as before about capturing the visiting boy. About the time for the boy to make his appearance, the father hid himself behind the side of the entrance and turned into a piece of straw. When the visiting boy arrived, he called, and his brother invited him in again. He looked around in the grass lodge, but didn't see anything this time. So he entered and ate with his brother. The father had told his boy that when his brother came he should get him to look into his hair for lice, then the boy was to look in the visiting boy's hair. While he was looking, he was to tie his hair so that the father could get a good hold on it. Then he was to call his father. After eating they both went out to begin their game. They played until the visiting boy won all his brother's arrows. When they stopped, the boy asked his brother if they couldn't look into each other's hair for lice. The visiting boy agreed and looked into his brother's hair first. Then he allowed his brother to look into his hair. While the boy was looking into his hair the visiting boy asked him what he was doing. He said that he was having a hard time parting the hair. When he got a good hold of the visiting boy's hair, he called his father. The visiting boy dragged him a good ways before the father reached them. Even when the old man got hold, the boy was so strong that he dragged both the father and the brother toward the river. But the father begged him to stop. They finally released the visiting boy, and he jumped in the water and came out again with his arms full of arrows. They started back towards their home. This visiting boy was named Afterbirth Boy. His brother was Lodge Boy.

After that, Afterbirth Boy began to dwell with his father and brother. When their father would go out hunting the boys would go out and shoot birds. When the father was home, he forbid the boys to go to four places --- one on the north, where a woman lived; one on the east, where the Thunderbird lived in a nest in a high tree; one on the south, where Double-Faced Man lived. He also made the boys a hoop and told them not to roll it toward the west. It was a long time before the boys desired to go abroad, but after a time, when the father was hunting, Afterbirth Boy asked his brother to go with him to visit the place in the north. Lodge Boy agreed, and they started off at once. On their way they shot a good many birds which they carried along with them. When they arrived they saw smoke. The old woman who lived there was glad to get the birds and said that she always liked to eat birds. Then she asked the boys to go to the creek and bring her a potful of water. She told the boys she had to put the birds in the water and boil them before she could eat them. So the boys went to the creek and brought the water. When they returned, the woman hung the pot of water over the fire, snatched the boys, and threw them in instead of the birds. The water began to boil, and Afterbirth Boy got on the side where the water was bubbling. He told his brother to make a quick leap while he did the same. They made a quick jump and poured the boiling water on the old woman, scalding her to death. When they had killed her, they started back home. They reached home before their father. When their father arrived, they told him they had visited the place in the north and about the dangers they had met at the home of the old woman, who was Little Spider Woman.

The next day they started to visit the Thunderbird. When they came to the place in the east they saw a high tree with the nest of the Thunderbird. Afterbirth Boy spoke to his brother saying, "Well, brother, take my arrows and I will climb the tree and see what sort of young ones these Thunderbirds have." He began to climb the tree, and all at once he heard thundering and saw a streak of lightning come down and take off his left leg. Afterbirth Boy told his brother to take care of his leg while he kept on climbing. When he began to climb higher, the bird came again. The thundering began and a streak of lightning came down and took off his left arm. Still he kept on, for he was anxious to get to the nest. He was near the nest when his right leg was taken off, so that he had just one arm left when he reached the nest. Now the Thunderbird did not bother him any more. He picked up one of the young ones and asked whose child he was. The young one replied he was the child of Weather-Followed-by-Hard-Winds and that sometimes he appeared as thunder and lightning. When the boy heard this he threw the bird down, saying that he was not the right kind of child. He told his brother to destroy him. Afterbirth Boy then took another bird, and asked him the same question. The young one replied he was the child of Clear-Weather-with-Sun-Rising-Slowly. He put the bird back in the nest, telling him he was a pretty good child. He took up another and asked whose child he was. The bird said he was the child of Cold-Weather-Following-Wind-and-Snow. Afterbirth Boy dropped him down and ordered his brother to put him to death. He then picked up the last bird and asked whose child he was. The young one answered that he was the child of Foggy-Day-Followed-by-Small-Showers. Afterbirth Boy put this child back in the nest, telling him he was the right kind of child. He then started to climb down the tree with his one arm. When he reached the ground, his brother put his right leg on him. Afterbirth Boy jumped around to see if it was all right. His brother then put on his left arm, and he swung that around to see if it was all right. Then the brother put on the left leg, and he felt just as good as he did when he first began to climb the tree. The two boys returned home before their father came back from his hunting. When their father came back, Afterbirth Boy began to tell what they had done while visiting the Thunderbirds and how his limbs were taken off. The boys laughed to think how Afterbirth Boy had looked with one arm and both legs off. The father began to think that his boy had great powers, and he didn't say much more to the boys about going to dangerous places.

Some time after, the boys went out again and came to the place in the south where their mother was put after her death. They saw a stone in the shape of a human being, and they both lay on it. When they started to get up, they found that they were stuck to it. They both made an effort and managed to get up still stuck to the stone. They took it home for their father to use for sharpening his stone knife. When they reached home the old man told them to take the stone back where they had found it. He told them that it was their mother. She had turned to stone after her death. They took the stone back where they had found it.

Later, Afterbirth Boy and his brother started out to the forbidden place where Double-Faced Man who had killed their mother lived. The Double-Faced creatures were living in a cave. When the boys arrived at the cave, Double-Faced Man's children came out and scratched the boys. If there was any blood on their fingers they would put them in their mouths. Afterbirth Boy took the string of his bow and killed the young ones. He caught the old Double-Faced Man and tied his bowstring around his neck so that he could take him home to his father to have in place of a dog. When they returned home, the old man walked out and seeing Double-Faced Man told the boys to take him off and kill him. They did.

Every day they played, as they had done before, going out to shoot birds and roll their hoop. Afterbirth Boy said to his brother, "Let's roll the hoop toward the west and see what happens." They rolled it toward the west, and it began going faster and faster. The boys kept running after it until they were going so fast they could not stop. They kept going faster, until they ran into the water where the hoop rolled. When they went into the water they fell into the mouth of a water monster, and he swallowed them. It seemed to them as though they were in a tipi, for the ribs of the monster reminded them of tipi poles. They wondered how they could get out. Afterbirth Boy took his bowstring with his right hand, drew it through his left hand to stretch it, and then swung it around and around. When he first swung it, the monster moved. He swung the string a second time, and the monster began to move more. He swung it a third time, and the monster moved still more. At this point, Afterbirth Boy told his brother that their father was getting uneasy about them and that they must get out of the monster at once. They had been away from home a long time. Again he swung his bowstring, and the monster jumped so high he fell on dry land. He opened his mouth, and the boys quickly stepped out and started for home.

When they arrived at the lodge, they found no one. Their father had gone off somewhere, but they couldn't find out where. Afterbirth Boy looked all around for a trail, but couldn't find any trace. At last he grew weary and decided to wait till night to look for their father. When night came, Afterbirth Boy looked around some more to see where their father had gone. He finally found the trail, and he followed it with his eye until he found the place where his father had stopped. He called his brother and told him to bring his arrows and to shoot them right up over his head. The brother brought the arrows and shot one straight up into the sky. Then he waited for awhile. Finally he saw a drop of blood come down. It was the blood of their father. When the boys did not return, he gave up all hope of seeing them again. So he went up into the sky and became a star. They knew that this blood belonged to their father, and in this way they found out where he had gone. Then they shot two more arrows straight up. They caught hold of these arrows and went up with them. Now the two brothers stand beside their father as stars in the sky.

13. LOON-WOMAN

(Shasta)

A mother and her ten children were living together. The oldest was a girl called Loon-Woman. She was mean; and her mother had to hide the youngest child, a boy called Floats-up-in-air, from her. Loon-Woman used to ask her mother, "Where is that child you had some time ago?" to which her mother used to reply, "Oh, I lost him some time ago." Every morning Loon-Woman saw her mother go down to the spring. She followed her and noticed that the water was disturbed, as if someone had been swimming there.

One day Loon-Woman found a long hair in the water. She measured it with the hairs of her other brothers, and found it to be too long. So she decided to learn whose hair it was. Every night she camped at the spring, until one morning she saw a strange man come down to bathe. Then she knew who had been disturbing the water and to whom the hair belonged. It was Floats-up-in-air. She fell in love with her brother and decided to marry him.

She went home and asked her mother to prepare some food for her as she was going away. Her mother gave her food, and Loon-Woman asked, "Who wants to accompany me?" The oldest brother said, "I." "No," she replied, "not you." And so she refused to go with any of her other brothers. Finally, she ran to the side of the house, put her hand there, and said, "This is the one I want to take along." Then Floats-up-in-air came out from where he had been hidden all these years and said, "All right, I'll go with you." They travelled all day. When night came, Loon-Woman said, "Let's stop here!" So they stopped there, and the girl began to prepare the bed. Floats-up-in-air suspected that she wanted him to sleep with her, but he said nothing. He only wished that she might fall sound asleep, so he could run away from her. After awhile she fell sound asleep. He put a log in her arms and left her, returning to the house. He ran home, shouting, "Let's all get ready to come with me." They did so, and before departing cautioned everything in the house not to tell Loon-Woman where they had gone. But they forgot to tell Ashes.

Early in the morning Loon-Woman woke up and began to speak to the log, thinking it to be her husband. But soon she found out that she had been deceived. She jumped up furious and cried, "I'll kill you for this!"

In the meantime, Floats-up-in-air and his family climbed in a basket and were being drawn up into the sky. Loon-Woman came home and inquired of everything in the house where her mother and brothers had gone. No one would tell. Finally, she asked Ashes. Ashes said they had gone up into the sky. She looked up and saw her family halfway up to the sky. She began to weep and called for them to come back down. But Floats-up-in-air had told them not to look back, no matter how often she might call. Soon, however, the mother looked back, and the basket began to fall. Loon-Woman was glad when she saw the basket coming down. She made a big fire and intended to kill her family as soon as the basket should fall into it. The basket fell down, but when Floats-up-in-air hit the ground, he flew right up and floated away. Loon-Woman thought that she had killed them all. She took their hearts and hung them about her neck and was glad.

After awhile Floats-up-in-air came down on the ocean beach, where two Sea-Gull girls found him. At first the girls were afraid of him, but he assured them, saying, "Don't be afraid of me! Touch me, wash me, and you will find that I am all right!" The girls did as directed, and Floats-up-in-air married them. After a while his wives became pregnant and gave birth to a boy and a girl. As soon as the children grew up, Floats-up-in-air gave them a bow and arrow, and taught them how to shoot, saying, "When you grow up, I want you to go to my sister over yonder and watch her secretly." The children grew up and went to their aunt's house, who scared them so that they ran back in a hurry. Then Floats-up-in-air said to his children. "Let's go and kill my sister! She is mean. She killed my family." The children promised to help him.

So they all went. Floats-up-in-air began to fight with his sister, but he could not kill her, because the only vulnerable spot, her heart, was in the soul of her foot. He shot arrow after arrow into her. He could not kill her. His arrows were all gone, and he was almost exhausted, when Meadow-Lark came to his help. She told him to look at Loon-Woman's heel. He did so and saw something bright and shining. He shot an arrow at it and thus was successful in killing the terrible Loon-Woman.

14. COYOTE KILLS THE SUCKING MONSTER

(Flathead)

From Spokane Falls Coyote came up to Ravalli. There he met an Old Woman, who was camped close to where Ravalli Station is now. The Old Woman said to Coyote, "Where are you going?" --- "Oh," said Coyote, "I am going to travel all over the world." --- "Well," said the Old Woman, "you had better go back from here." --- "Why should I go back from here?" asked Coyote. --- "Because there is a Giant in this valley who kills everyone that goes through," replied the Old Woman. --- "Well," said Coyote, "I will fight with him and kill him."

Then Coyote started on the trail again. He saw a great big tamarack tree growing on the hillside, and he pulled it up and threw it over his shoulder and went on his way. He said to himself, "I'll choke that Giant with this tamarack tree. That's what I'll do." Pretty soon he saw a woman that was nearly dead. "What is the matter with you?" asked Coyote. "Are you sick?" --- The woman said, "No, I am not sick." --- Coyote said, "I am going to choke the Giant with this tamarack tree." --- The woman said, "You might as well throw that stick away. Don't you know you are already in the Giant's belly?" Then Coyote threw the tamarack against the hillside. It can now be seen close to Arlee, a little station on the Northern Pacific Railroad. It stuck against the hillside and grew. All of what is now Jacko Valley was filled by the Giant's belly.

Coyote went on from there, and he saw lots of people lying around. Some of them were dead, and some were pretty nearly dead. "What is the matter with you people?" asked Coyote. They all said, "We are starving to death." --- Coyote said, "What makes you starve? There is plenty to eat in here, lots of meat and fat?" Then Coyote cut chunks of grease from the sides of the Giant and fed them to the people, who got better. And then Coyote said, "Now, all of you people get ready to run out. I am going to cut the Giant's heart. When I start to cut you must all run out at O'Keef's Canyon or over at Ravalli."

The Giant's heart was the rounded cluster of mountains north of Flathead Agency, and there are marks on the side which show the place that Coyote cut with his stone knife. Coyote began to cut the Giant's heart. Pretty soon the Giant said, "Please, Coyote, let me alone. You go out. I don't want you to stay in here. You can go out." --- Coyote said, "No, I won't go out. I am going to

stay right here. I am going to kill you." Then he started to cut
the Giant's heart. He cut the Giant's heart off and then ran out.
The Giant was dying, and his jaws began to close. Woodtick was
the last to come out. The Giant's jaws were just closing down
on him when Coyote caught him and pulled him out. "Well," said
Coyote, "you will always be flat. I can't help it now. You must
be flat." That is the reason Woodtick is so flat.

15. WALKING SKELETON

(Western Mono)

The people were about to play hand games in the house.
Walking Skeleton was travelling towards the house. He was climbing the mountain ridge below, just at dawn. He was singing. The
people in the house were getting ready to play hand games and were
kindling for their fire. The opposing groups played on opposite
sides of the fire. At this point, Walking Skeleton appeared. "What
are those people doing?" he asked as he put his head in the door
and whistled. All of the people died, because they looked at Walking
Skeleton when he whistled.

The people in the house had previously sent a girl outside
of the house as a lookout. She put on a rabbit-skin blanket when
she went outside as a guard. She had not seen the approach of
Walking Skeleton. Consequently, when she returned to the house
she was astonished to find everyone dead. The only person who
was alive was a little girl who had been asleep and who had not
looked at Walking Skeleton or heard him whistle. The child awoke
at sunrise, and the girl who had been on guard opened the door for
her to go out. When they were together outside, the older girl
began to cry and sob, "What am I going to do all by myself in
this world?" Finally she said to the child, "We will have to leave,"
and she began to gather what food she could. She did not want
to leave her house at once, so she went about tidying things and
going back and forth. "What will we do now?" she asked, taking
the child by the hand. "You gamblers certainly look fine now,"
she said to the dead. After taking the things she wanted, she set
fire to the house and cremated the dead people. Then she and the
child started off.

The girl started on her wanderings, but she hadn't gone far
when she thought of some pine nuts near the house. She went back
for them, and after getting them started off again with the child
and a large bundle. After they had gone halfway to the ridge, the
child became exhausted. The girl decided to camp there beside

the trail. She left the child and went to dig some potatoes. She gathered a basketful, made a fire, and roasted them in the ashes. This took up a lot of time. Finally the two sat down to eat. The girl kept looking about her, fearing that Walking Skeleton might still be around. Sure enough, he came along and sat down between the girl and the child.

"Eat some potatoes with us," said the girl. "I surely will eat some," answered Walking Skeleton. "They taste nice." --- "Just help yourself," replied the girl, and she went off to dig some more of them. She looked back when she got on the ridge and said, "What am I going to do with myself now?" She looked about and saw a rock pile that might serve as a refuge. Then she walked back to the ridge and took another look below at Walking Skeleton, because she thought she smelled something roasting. She saw that the little girl had disappeared, and she noted that Walking Skeleton was licking blood from a rock. When Walking Skeleton had finished, he called to the girl, "Your child is crying." She called back, "I'll be there in a few minutes."

Walking Skeleton called to her again, but she hid behind a clump of bushes. She said, "I will leave an echo here, so that when he calls it will answer him. I had better get to a safer place." She went to the edge of the ridge and looked over once more. Walking Skeleton was going through the bundle which she had been carrying. She stood there and watched him. Then she started on her journey. She crossed two ridges, then she said, "I'll have to travel faster." So she took a long pole, pressed one end of it against the ground and vaulted over a high mountain. About this time, Walking Skeleton started to track her.

Beyond the mountain, she found a sage bush growing beside a big rock. She pulled the bush up by the roots and hid herself in the hole beside the rock; then she put the bush back. About sundown Walking Skeleton reached the girl's hiding place. He dug around the bush a bit, then he said, "I think I will wait till morning. I will sit up all night so she can't escape." He burned some logs, so he would have plenty of light. He lay there and kept turning and turning. "I wish it were morning," he said, because he was tired of waiting. The girl heard him all night long and was weary. "I don't know what I will do. I am afraid my end is near." However, at dawn Walking Skeleton was sound asleep.

The girl heard his snoring and said to herself, "He's sound asleep. I don't think he can catch me if I leave now." When she came out she stood right above him and looked at him while he was sound asleep. She left and crossed two ridges before Walking Skeleton awoke. When he awoke he looked around for a minute or two, then he began to dig up the sage bush, hoping to eat the girl for his breakfast. As he pulled the bush up by the root, he turned over and fell to pieces. His parts came together again, and he exclaimed, "Why did I sleep? My fresh meat has escaped."

Walking Skeleton again set out in pursuit of the fleeing girl and about sundown he overtook her. She went into a cave. He went on by it, without realizing that she was so near. When he had passed, the girl set out for the camp of her mother's brothers, Wolf and Coyote, who lived near-by. Wolf, the older brother, had sent Coyote to the spring for a basket of water. There Coyote saw the girl. He ran back to camp, telling Wolf, "Why, elder brother, there is a very pretty girl at the spring." --- "All right," said Wolf, "I will go and see her." He told Coyote to keep behind him, but Coyote ran on ahead. When Wolf arrived, Coyote said, "I got here first. I want to marry this girl." Wolf said, "Stop that sort of talk," then he asked the girl, "My sister's daughter, how did you come here?" The girl explained, then asked, "How are you two going to help me? Walking Skeleton is close behind me." Wolf replied, "I am afraid we can't do anything for you. However, I have a big pelt in which you can hide. I will wrap you in it." The two brothers wrapped the girl and placed her on a platform in a tree." Soon Walking Skeleton appeared.

"I want you to give me that girl; I know she is here," said Walking Skeleton. "We don't know anything about her," said Wolf and Coyote. "I tracked her to your camp," Walking Skeleton went on. "We like fresh meat ourselves," said the brothers. Walking Skeleton kept walking about, getting closer and closer to the girl's hiding place. "I think I will stay here all night, he said; so he had a meal with the brothers. They brought out two pelts for him to sleep on. Wolf said aside to Coyote, "Younger brother, we will not sleep tonight. I do not like the looks of this man." Coyote made no reply; he just rolled his eyes.

After Walking Skeleton had gone to sleep, the two brothers roasted trout for the girl. They wrapped them in tule and took them to her. "You had better leave now, while he is fast asleep. We cannot do anything against him. When you eat this fish, drink water with it." The girl departed. When she had climbed to the top of the neighboring ridge, she paused to look down into the canyon below.

When Walking Skeleton awoke, he said to Wolf and Coyote, "You had better give me that girl. There is no use for you to try to conceal her from me." "What are you going to do with her if we give her to you," asked the brothers. "Oh, I shall take her home, and she will wait on me and get water for me." Once he had discovered that his quarry had escaped, Walking Skeleton went back to tracking her.

Meanwhile the girl had pushed back into the mountains and reached the camp of an aunt who was named Joined-to-Willow. She was named this because she was continually scraping willow bark for basket-making. "Aunt, can you help me? Walking Skeleton is right behind me. Where can you hide me?" asked the girl. --- "I am afraid I can't do much for you. I will do the best I can; I will put you somewhere for the night." So she placed the girl in a burden basket and covered her with tule roots. She then put the basket back among her other baskets. The girl had not been hidden long when Walking Skeleton arrived. He said to himself, "It is useless for me to track further, for I know the girl is right here. This time I am going to capture her." He stayed all night at the woman's camp and slept soundly. Towards daybreak the old woman went to the girl and said, "You had better leave now, for he is sound asleep." The girl took her aunt's advice and departed.

At daybreak, Walking Skeleton was again on her trail, exclaiming to himself, "Ah, here is her track." However, the girl reached Skunk's house before her pursuer caught her. "What are you going to do for me?" she asked. Skunk owned a lot of pitch. He said, "I will help you." He heated the pitch so that it became very sticky. Then he put it in holes dug in the trail over which Walking Skeleton was coming. Walking Skeleton came hurrying along the road. He stepped into the holes that Skunk had prepared for him and disappeared beneath the surface of the pitch. He died this way.

The girl walked about Skunk's place for awhile. She was very grateful for having escaped. She said to Skunk, "What a wonderful thing you did in catching Walking Skeleton." After a time she decided to travel to Eagle's home. As her pursuer was dead, she stopped to admire the beautiful things in Eagle's country. "What beautiful flowers there are in this country," she thought, "and how pretty the stars are at night. This is the life." Finally, she reached Eagle's house. As she stood on top of a cliff she looked out over the whole country. "Well, this country looks like an ocean. This is the best part of the world I have ever been in. I am smiling all over with joy."

Eagle brought home a deer. He greeted his visitor. She returned his greeting. Then Eagle went in and made a fire. He invited the girl into his house, as it was cold outside. "There is room for you on one side there," he said. "Keep yourself warm." He began to skin the deer he had brought. After he had finished he came in and put the pot on the fire to make stew. When it was done, he said, "Come now, we will have our meal. You can have the pot of stew." He gave her the pot, taking out a small piece of meat for himself. "All right. This is quite a treat for me," said the girl. Then Eagle said, "You must sleep in the same corner you are sitting in. Sleep right there. Tomorrow night you may move your bed a little closer to my bed." --- "All right," said the girl. Then Eagle said, "We will have intercourse in ten days, but not before."

Nevertheless, in two days the girl bore two children, and in a few days a big band of children had been born. "Now we are getting too many," said Eagle. "We had better pair them off. My wife, we will pair them off and name them. They will be different tribes of people." He began to pair them off. "This pair will be Miwok. This pair we will call Chukchansi. This pair we will call Mono." Then he sent all the pairs out. "Now you establish homes and settle down. This will make the world. You people increase; the world looks too bare. Fill it."

All went out to their places. They all went away happy. Eagle looked over the cliff himself to see them start. "How beautiful it is to see people walking," he said. "The world certainly looks nice." Then he turned to the girl and said, "Now we are going to kill deer, as I did when we first met. We are only two now, paired off."

Part 2

WHAT MAN MUST KNOW AND LEARN

Famine was a continual threat to the American Indian. Thus, hunting and primitive agriculture loomed large in his mind. It is only natural to find a host of tales which relate to food and to times when food was impossible to get. The story of Bloodclot, the youth who is miraculously born from buffalo blood, and the story of Sweet Medicine, the man whose name literally translated would mean "Sweet-standing-root", both tell of hard times and heroes who saved the day. The Bloodclot story, which is well-known to the Plains tribes and to the California tribes, often includes further adventures much like those of Afterbirth Boy and Lodge Boy. It should be read in comparison with that story and with Tale 18, Yellowtop-to-Head Woman, which covers very similar ground.

Tale 19, The Origin of Corn, was pretty standard among the woodland tribes of the East. The maiden is usually slain before she is dragged across the ground, though that is not evident in the text printed here.

16. BLOODCLOT

(Southern Ute)

Long ago a very old man and his wife were staying by themselves. They were hunting game but could not get enough food. The man found some buffalo tracks. He saw where the buffalo had stopped, looked, and found a big clot of blood. He took off his shirt and carried the clot home in it. He told his wife to boil the blood. She said, "I'll get water." She went to the creek, put the water into a kettle, and began to boil it. When it was not yet boiling hot, a baby was heard crying in the kettle. She told her husband to take it out quickly. He ran and did so. They washed it and wrapped up the little boy into which the clot had been changed. The old people did not know how the baby had come to be there; they could not find out about it. The next morning the baby had grown much larger and continued to grow till he could crawl about by himself. The following day he was able to walk a little. The next day he walked about. Every day he grew. The old man made arrows for him and he began to shoot. As he grew he made him larger arrows. The boy shot birds and other small game.

The boy said to the old man, "I have killed something with a striped back." He never brought the game home himself, but would send the old man for it. This time it was an animal a little bigger than a mouse. The old man cooked it, and the three ate it. Every day the boy went out. The next time he said, "I have killed a white short-tailed animal." It was a cottontail. The old man cooked it and all three ate it. The next day he went far off and killed a badger. "I have killed an animal in a hole in the ground." They got it, cooked it and ate. The next day he went out again and when he returned he said, "I have killed an animal with black ears and a black tail." They found a female deer. The old man was glad now. He brought it home, and they ate it and were happy. The next day Bloodclot went out and killed an elk. "I have killed a big fellow with big antlers." The old man found it and brought it home, and again they had enough meat. The old man gave the boy a big bow and arrows. He went into the mountains and killed a mountain-goat. "I have killed an animal with big horns in the mountains." The old man brought the mountain-goat home. "Every day," he said, "he kills a different kind of animal." Now their troubles were over; they had an easy time

of it. The next day the boy killed a mountain lion. The following day he killed an otter. "I have killed an animal with nice fur,
living in the water." The old man tanned the skin to be used for
strings to tie the boy's braids. The next day the boy said, "I have
killed a water-animal with a bare tail of this size." It was a
beaver. Now they were never short of fresh meat.

Finally Bloodclot said: "I want to visit the camp. Before
that I will go on my last hunt for you. I'll be gone all day and
all night. First I want you to tie up the tent, put rocks on the
edge, and fasten the door lest the wind at night carry it away.
There will be a big wind, but don't go outdoors and don't be afraid.
I'll call when you are to come out." The old couple obeyed. He
stayed out all night while they were sleeping. About daybreak they
heard a big noise and a wind was coming as if to tip over the
tent. The old man was frightened and wanted to run out but his
wife held him back. "Don't you remember what our son said?"
He was afraid the tent might fall, but she restrained him. Daylight
came, and their son's voice was heard saying, "Come out and look
here; I'll show you something." They unfastened the door and
stepped out. There were dead buffalo there. "I have done this
for you. Dry the meat and hides and save the meat." They got
busy and the boy asked his mother to fix a lunch for him. She
got him some nice pemmican. He had buckskin leggings and a
quiver of mountain-lion hide. "Now you parents have plenty of
food." They cried before he left and asked him to return.

Bloodclot went off and after a few days he reached the village, which was large. He walked to the edge of the camp and
met a man, whom he asked for the chief's house. "It is in the
center." He went there and found the chief, his wife and daughter
inside. They asked him to sit down and the chief asked where he
came from and what tribe he belonged to. "I don't know what tribe
I belong to; I have come to visit you." The chief stepped outdoors
and shouted to the people; to come and see their visitor. All came.
They sat there. The chief said, "Do any of you know the tribe of
this young man?" Then they asked him whether he belonged to the
Deer, Elk, Otters, Beavers, and so forth. None of them thought of
Buffalo till one old man said, "I think I know him slightly, though
I may be mistaken. I think he is one of the Buffalo." --- "Yes,
I am one of the Buffalo." Then the people said, "All right, we
want you to stay here and marry the chief's daughter." So he
married her.

That evening he told his father-in-law to get one arrow from
the tipi. When he returned, he told him to have all the tipis fastened and to tell all the people to stay indoors. He prophesied a

big storm. The chief told all the people. They obeyed. At day-break they heard a big noise and began to shout but none went out. Then came a big wind, but it lasted only a short time. They heard a voice outdoors telling the chief to step out. Then the chief saw dead buffalo before every lodge. Bloodclot told him to call the other people for a feast. He did so, and all were happy over the buffalo. They had been starving to death.

For a while Bloodclot lived with those people. One day they went buffalo hunting. He told his wife that she was not to use the word "calf". They went out. He was with his wife. They killed some buffalo and were butchering when another herd came running. His wife yelled for him to kill a calf. "Kill that calf!" she said. He immediately got on his horse and ran off as a buffalo. She cried and tried to catch him, but he went with the buffalo.

17. THE STORY OF SWEET MEDICINE

(Cheyenne)

Once, a long time ago, a baby was born. They used to wrap it in its covering and leave it in the lodge. Sometimes at night, when they went to bed, the baby was gone. Only its wrappings would be there. In the morning, when they arose, the baby was there again. It grew, and after a while was so large that it could walk and run about a little.

The boy's father and mother had died while he was little. A poor old woman took care of him as best she could and reared him. He was very poor and had only a small piece of buffalo-robe to wear. He used to sleep wherever he could, most of the time out in the brush. He had strange ways about sleeping. Sometimes he would lie down to sleep anywhere, and, if people tried to wake him, they found they could not do so. It would seem as if he were dead. So the people used to say, "Let him alone. Do not wake him. Let him wake up himself."

As he grew larger, he was often mischievous, and some people did not like him. Once an old woman's dog was dragging a travois. The boy kept putting his foot on one of the poles and holding it back. Then the old woman grew angry and abused him, saying, "What are you doing? Who are you, anyhow? You have no father." She called him bad names.

In this old time the people used to come together and dance. One day the boy asked his grandmother if he could dance too.

"No", said his grandmother, "you had better wait. This dance is a religious one. You cannot go to it, you are too small." The boy kept teasing to go. He teased and teased, and at last he cried and said he wanted to go.

"Well", said his grandmother, "you can go. How do you want to be dressed and painted?"

The boy was wearing a little calf-skin robe. The hair of the robe was still red. He said to his grandmother, "I want my body to be painted yellow, in stripes, and my robe to be painted white. I want the feather I wear on my head to be yellow, and the bow-string that I shall wear about my neck to be yellow also."

The old woman asked, "Why do you want to wear a bowstring about your neck?"

The boy said, "I want it so that I can take my head off my body".

His grandmother said to him, "Are you telling the truth?" And the boy replied, "Yes. After my head is off my body, place the head close to the body, and lay the head toward the rising sun, and cover me with my calf-robe." The old woman thought the boy was only going to choke himself; but the boy repeated again what he had said -- that she should place his head and body toward the rising sun, and cover it with the robe, and then should take up the robe and shake it four times.

The boy was dressed as he asked, and the old-woman went with him to the lodge where the dance was going on. There was a great crowd about the lodge; and when they got there the old woman spoke to those who were looking on, saying, "Make room for us to pass, so that we may go in." The people moved to one side, and they entered the lodge. When they entered, the medicine-man who had charge of the dance said, "Why, here is Sweet Medicine come to dance! Come over here and sit down by me." Sweet Medicine went over to the back of the lodge and sat down at the right of the medicine-man, and for a time sat there watching the people dance.

The dance went on, but from time to time they stopped and rested and talked. Sweet Medicine's robe lay close by him. To-ward the last part of the dance he arose and danced about, hold-ing the bowstring around his neck in both hands. At the last part of the dance, just before they were about to eat, he pulled the bow-string tight. It cut off his head, which fell to the ground, but his body continued to dance. Those who were looking on called out, "Why, Sweet Medicine has cut his head off!"

The body kept on dancing; and the head rolled about on the ground, and every now and then it looked up at the people. When they stopped dancing, the body fell down, and the old woman walked over and put the body and head together, and placed the bowstring by the boy's side, and took the calf-skin robe off and shook it four times. Then she put it back over Sweet Medicine, took the bowstring and wiped it off four times, and placed it on the ground by his side. When she had done this, Sweet Medicine arose with a smile on his face.

Sweet Medicine did this to show the people what he was. He did this once, so that all the people might know what he could do. He always wore one of the under-plumes of an eagle's wing tied to his hair.

Sweet Medicine grew up to be a young man. He always wore his feather and a calf-skin robe with the hair side out. When he had become a young man, no one paid much attention to him or thought much about him.

Once he went to war against some people and was shot in the back with an arrow. His companions wished to pull the arrow out; but he said, "No, leave it. I will let my grandmother pull it out, so that she can see it." One night, when they were on the way home, he sat by the fire with his head down, saying nothing. Those who were with him wondered what he was thinking about. As they sat there, they saw a few ants run out from the hole where the arrow stuck in his body, and then run back again. They whispered to each other, "He must be a great man; he must have power."

When they had come near the village, he said to one of the young men, "Go into the village and tell my grandmother that I am coming, but that I am wounded." When they told the old woman this, she went out to meet her grandson, singing a song. When she met him, she pulled the arrow out of his wound, and he went with her into the camp. He grew to be a man and stayed with the people.

One day they had surrounded the buffalo and had killed many. This young man had killed a fat two-year-old bull, with a robe as black as charcoal. He skinned the bull, and left the head, legs, and even the hoofs, on the hide. After he had done this, he spread it out, hair side up, and stood with his friend, looking at it and thinking how pretty it was. While they were looking at it, a great chief came up to them. "Ha!" he said, "that is just the kind of a robe I have been looking for. It is just what I want. I will take it."

"No," said Sweet Medicine, "I need the robe, and that is why I killed him; but he is nice and fat, and you can have the meat."

"No", said the chief, "I want the robe."

"That is what I want", said the boy, "Many other buffaloes have been killed. Go take a robe from one of those. I want this for my own use. But you can have the meat."

The chief grew angry and said, "How dare you talk back to me!" He drew his knife and ran to the hide and cut it into small pieces. Then the young man was angry. He caught up the bone of the buffalo's hind-leg and struck the chief on the head and killed him. Then he went back to camp.

By the time he had reached his lodge, every one knew that he had killed the chief. The soldiers were angry. They said, "We will kill him. We will beat him to death." His grandmother ran to the lodge where he was sitting and said to him, "Run, run! the soldiers are coming." Sweet Medicine said to her, "Go away! You trouble me." The soldiers gathered about the lodge. When they entered to take him, he upset a pot of water that was standing on the fire and rose out of the smokehole with the steam and ashes. The soldiers tore the lodge down, but could not find him. While they were looking for him, one of them saw him sitting on a little hill not far from camp. They rushed over there to catch him; but when they had come to the hill, he was not there. Still they kept watching for him.

One day a man was out looking over the country, and near a great cut bluff he saw a little smoke. Looking down below, he saw Sweet Medicine among the thick bushes at the foot of the bluff, roasting meat over a little fire. When they learned of this, the soldiers went out and surrounded the place. When they had done so, they ran into the bushes, calling out, "Rush on him and kill him! Aha! now we have got you!" They all rushed forward, and a coyote ran out of the bushes by them. They said, "Why, a coyote was in there too!" They looked everywhere for Sweet Medicine, but could not find him. They found his meat on a stick up where it was roasting. They then knew the coyote must have been Sweet Medicine.

Another time he was found in a similar place. A man saw him and told of it. They surrounded the place and rushed in to seize him, and a magpie flew out and alighted on a hill, and made a great chattering; but Sweet Medicine was gone.

Again a man saw him on a canyon with high bluffs all about. Again he was roasting meat. They surrounded the place, and began to come together, and to shout that now they had him. A crow flew out and alighted on the bank, but Sweet Medicine was gone. They thought that he might have hidden himself among the thick overhanging willows, and searched for him; but he was not there.

A fourth time they found him in a similar place, and he looked up and smiled at them. They surrounded the place, and again began to shout and say, "Now we will beat him to death." When they rushed in, a blackbird flew out and lighted on the bluff, and looked down, chirping at the crowd. They could not find Sweet Medicine; and some said, "Look carefully among those matted vines and that thick grass. Perhaps he is there." They did not find him.

Again he was seen, and they surrounded the place with a double line; as they rushed in, an owl flew out and alighted on the ground above, and watched them.

One day, after all this had happened, Sweet Medicine was seen standing close to the camp. He was finely dressed, with feathers in his head, a rattle in his hand, and wearing a long shoulder-belt that looked as if it were ornamented with porcupine-quills, -- a dog rope. The soldiers ran to catch him, and he ran away. While they could see him, he ran slowly, and they almost caught him; but when he passed over the hill, he ran very fast. When they next saw him, he was a long way ahead. They could not catch him.

The next day he was seen again, dressed differently. He wore a bonnet of buffalo-hide, and a belt strung with buffalo-tails hanging down, and rattles on his moccasins, and carried in his hand a lance that he used as a cane. When he was first seen, he was walking about outside the circle. When they saw him, they called out, "There is Sweet Medicine!" and rushed toward him. He did as he had done before. While they could see him, he ran as if exhausted; but when hidden from sight, he ran fast. At last they became tired out and left him.

The next day he came in a different dress. He wore a war-bonnet and carried a crooked-lance in his hand. All happened as before.

The fourth day he painted himself black all over. He carried a lance like that now used in the Fox dance. All things happened as before.

On the fifth day he wore an owl headdress and bull-hide moc-casin, with the long beard of a bull attached to the heels and drag-ging behind, and carried a lance. The same things took place that had happened on previous days.

The next day he came differently dressed. His face was painted. He carried a pipe and tobacco-sack and was acting like a chief. He sat down on a hill, and they rushed on him. Before they reached him, he walked over the hill; and when they came in sight of him, he was on the next hill. They gave him up then and decided that they would try a different plan to catch him.

One day they heard a great rumbling sound beyond a hill near the camp; and as they looked, they saw an animal come over the hill. As it drew nearer, it was a different animal from what they had thought at first; and then it changed to another animal; and at last it was Sweet Medicine, playing the wheel-game, and running close to the camp, as if to tempt them to pursue him. The people were all afraid and said to one another, "Do not trouble him." When he saw that they did not try to take him, he went back the way he had come and disappeared over the hill. The rumbling grew fainter as he moved away. They think that he came, intending to have destroyed the people if they had tried to take him.

One day they went to his brother and said to him, "Your brother may come back now; we will not harm him. He may come back; we will not hurt him. But when he comes back, you must take him out hunting, and kill a buffalo, and pile up the meat, and leave Sweet Medicine there to keep the flies off it while you return to camp to get the dogs. Then we will all move off and leave him!"

One night Sweet Medicine decided to go to his home, and he went to his brother's lodge, and entered. His brother said to him, "Is that you, brother? Come in and sit down." He said to his wife, "Give him food." She did so, and Sweet Medicine ate. A number of men had seen him come in and went to the lodge and told Sweet Medicine that no one would harm him. After he had eaten, he went to bed.

The next morning his brother asked him to go hunting. They started; and while they were gone the camp moved. The brother killed a buffalo, cut, up the meat nicely and heaped it together in a pile, and told Sweet Medicine to walk about the meat and keep the flies off while he went home for the dogs, so they could pack in the meat. The brother went to where the camp had been and followed it. Sweet Medicine stayed by the meat, keeping the flies away. At night he lay down by the pile and slept.

The tribe moved and moved; but they could find no game and came near starving. They could get no food, but were obliged to eat whatever they could, -- roots, the bark of trees, even mushrooms. It was a hard time. Everyone was hungry. After they had been gone for one winter, they thought that perhaps there might be some buffalo, at least some old bulls at the old camp. When they had come to the place, the brother of Sweet Medicine went out to see if he could find him. He did find him. Sweet Medicine was still walking about the pile of white bones where the meat had been, and about them he had worn a trail so deep that only the top of his head could be seen. His brother felt very sorry, and cried and mourned for Sweet Medicine, but Sweet Medicine did not speak to him. His brother could hear him talking to himself, saying, "I guess by this time my brother has become a great chief."

The brother went back to the village and told the people that his brother was still alive, but would not speak to him. The next day others of Sweet Medicine's relations went out to see him, but they did not find him; he was gone. They looked for him everywhere, -- in the hills, and in the timber -- but they could not find him.

Now, when Sweet Medicine went away, he went to some great place where he got his power and remained away for four years. The buffaloes and all the animals disappeared, and the people began to starve. All that they had to live on were such things as they could gather from the ground -- roots, berries, grass -- anything that they could pick up. They wandered and hunted all over the land, eating whatever they could find -- rosebuds, mushrooms, or the inner bark of trees. They would be gone from camp for two or three days, searching for mushrooms, and would bring in a little pack of them, which would soon be gone. As time went on, they grew more and more hungry. At last all were becoming so weak that they could hardly travel -- the people mere skin and bone; the children helpless from starvation and unable to walk.

One day, as the camp was moving along, seven little boys -- two of them small, and the other larger -- were travelling along off to one side of the camp. They were all hungry. As they went along they found some large white mushrooms. They began to pull and eat them. While they were sitting there eating the mushrooms, a man walked up to them. They looked around and suddenly saw him standing close to them. He was tall and good-looking and had long hair hanging loose way down his back.

He looked at the little boys for a time, and then said to them, "Why little boys, you seem to be very hungry. Are you starving?" The little boys said to him, "Yes, it is a long time since we have had any meat, anything real to eat."

"Ah," he said, "poor little boys! you are starving. Those things that you have are not fit to eat. Throw them away, we shall find plenty of food."

The boys did not like to throw away the mushrooms, which were all they had to eat, but again he told them to do so, and they threw them away.

Buffalo-chips were lying all about where buffaloes had formerly been. The young man said to the boys, "You little boys go off now, and each one find a buffalo-chip and bring it to me".

While they were gone, he took a stick in his hand and broke it in two and put it on the ground. Immediately it began to burn. He had a fire. The boys soon brought him seven chips. He spread his robe on the ground and placed the chips brought him by the five large boys on the robe in a square, with one in the middle. The two brought by the two smallest boys he placed, one to the east, and one to the west, of the corners of the square. The four chips at the corners of the square represented the four cardinal points, and the middle one the sun. The two to the east and the west represented the rising sun and the setting sun.

Then he took the four corners of his robe, and folded them over so that the chips were in a bunch in the middle of the robe, and covered them up. Then with his hand he broke up the chips and crumbled them to powder. He unfolded and opened out his robe, and there lying in it was pounded meat and fat.

Then he said, "Now, you little boys come up here and eat. Eat as much as you want." They ate all they wanted, until they were satisfied. After they had finished, he said to them, "Now grease yourselves all over with fat -- grease your faces, your hands, and your whole bodies. You look all dried up, as if you had been out in the sun. If you cannot eat all this food, take what is left back to the camp with you. Now, you seven boys go to your camp and tell the people to put up their lodges in a circle and to leave an opening in the circle toward the rising sun. In the middle of this circle they must pitch a big lodge; and if they have no big one, tell them to take two or three lodges and make a big one from them. Tell them to have all the head men come together in that lodge; and if they have anything in the camp to smoke, let them have the pipes there filled. Say to them that I am he who has come back to them."

The boys went into the camp, tired and full, and went to sleep without telling the people what Sweet Medicine had said. In the morning the smallest of the boys remembered, and said, "O father! Sweet Medicine has come back, and gave us plenty to eat yesterday." Then he gave the message. His father did not quite believe him and sent a messenger to ask the older boys if this were true. They said, "Yes, that is true. We forgot to tell it."

The people sent for the chiefs and told them what the little boys had said; and the chiefs went over to the lodge of Sweet Medicine's brother to ask if he had heard of Sweet Medicine, who had sent good news to the camp. The brother said, "No, I have not seen him." At the head of the brother's bed, covered up with robes, a man was lying who had come in during the night. "Who is that person?" the chief asked. "I do not know," said the brother.

"He came in during the night." They woke the man; and when he sat up and took the robe from his head, it was Sweet Medicine. The chiefs asked him about the message that he had sent in; and he said "Yes, that is what I told the little boys. Now, put up a big double lodge and level the ground off nicely inside. When it is ready, send for me. Let the lodge face the sun." They did this, and he entered the lodge.

When he went to it, all the people were mourning and crying, asking him to take pity on them and help them to food. After he had gone in and sat down, he said, "Go and get an old buffalo-skull and put it in the opening in the circle." They did this, and he began to sing. As he sang, the head began to move toward them. When it got pretty close to them, it grunted. After it had grunted, he told some of the men to bring it in and have it put at the back of the lodge near the fire.

To those sitting there he said, "I have been gone four years. I know that you people are hungry and are starving because there are no buffaloes. I want you all to stay in this lodge for four days and four nights. I want to sing for four days and four nights. After I have sung two days and two nights, on the third night you will hear the buffalo coming. On the third morning there will be buffaloes in sight, a few to be seen here and there. The fourth night they will come closer; and on the fourth day, in the morning, they will come into the camp, and be all around this lodge."

It happened as he had said. He sang; and on the third night, while he was singing, singing, singing, they began to hear noises all about the camp -- the blowing and grunting of buffaloes. Early in the morning of the fourth day the buffaloes were all through the camp and about the lodge. He said to the people, "Now go out and kill food for yourselves, as much as you need. I will sit here and sing, and the buffalo will not run away. You can kill all you want here in the camp." They did as he had said and killed many buffaloes. After he saw that they had enough, he called out to them to stop, saying that they had enough; and those buffaloes that were alive, all walked out through the gap in the circle.

After Sweet Medicine had come back to the camp, the people lived better and had more to eat. When he told them the whole story of where he had been and what he had done, the chief of the tribe gave him his daughter, a very pretty girl, for his wife. But they were not yet married. The people fixed up a dog with a travois, and he and the girl started back for the great place. When he went back to this place -- a big lodge within a hill -- he entered; and the people in the lodge said, "Ah! here is our grandson come back again. Come in, and sit down at the back of the lodge."

The people who were in this lodge were all the things and beings that belong to this earth. There were persons and buffaloes and antelopes; all animals and birds, rocks, trees, bushes, and grass. All things that grow or exist upon the earth.

When Sweet Medicine entered the lodge, there were a number of people sitting there, four of whom seemed to be principal men. And besides, at the right of the door as he went in, sat a black man; at the left of the door, a brown man, very handsome; at the back of the lodge, to the left, was a white, good-looking man; to the right, at the back of the lodge, was a brown, well-built man. All these men were handsomer than any he had ever seen. They were not doing anything; they sat there.

After Sweet Medicine had been in the lodge for some time, the chief person spoke to him, saying, "Now choose one of these men to be yourself." Sweet Medicine looked about and thought. When he had entered the lodge, the man at the left of the door had caught his eye, and he had liked him; but still, before choosing, he looked about at all the others. All were handsome, and he liked them all. All were men that he would have been glad to resemble. The chief person seemed to be making signs to him with his lips that he should choose a particular man. But at last Sweet Medicine pointed to the man at the left of the door, and said, "I will be like that one."

There was a moment's pause, and then all who were sitting in the lodge gave a low groan, saying, "E-he-heh! showing that they were sorry for him, that he had made a mistake. When they said this, he looked around quickly and saw that the handsome white man was not there; but a great white, smooth stone stood in his place. He looked for the next man, and he was gone; but where he had sat, a tall slender weed-stalk was growing, one of those that the Cheyennes use to throw. The black man had changed to a smooth black stone, while the man whom he had chosen was a nice pretty weed as high as a man's knee, with green leaves and pretty flowers on it.

The chief person pointed to one of the stones and said, "You ought to have chosen that one. Then you would have lived to old age; and after you had grown old, you would have become young again always. You would not have died. That man there is a mere fish-bladder. If you had chosen either of those persons, "You would have lived forever." The chief spirit had placed these stones so that they might be the first things Sweet Medicine would see, hoping that he would choose one of them and live forever.

When Sweet Medicine made his choice, one of the people sitting in the lodge said, "That man is a fool", and rose and went out. The chief person said to Sweet Medicine, "Follow him; he has great power". Sweet Medicine and another went out and followed the man for a long, long time. It seemed as if they went all over the world, and at last they came back to the same place. Then they gave Sweet Medicine advice, and gave him the medicine-arrows, and told him that he should take them back to the tribe. They told him, too, of many of the things that afterward happened.

Then said the chief person, "Take these arrows with you and guard them carefully. They will be a great help to you for a long time. You will keep them until they will cease to be a help and will be of no more use to you." With the arrows he was given a coyote's skin to wrap the arrows in. The arrows were feathered with eagle-feathers, and he brought them out, wrapped in the coyote's skin. The feather that he wore in his head was from the eagle that had given the feathers for the arrows.

After they left the sacred place, the girl carried the arrows on her back, and they led the dog. As they drew near the camp, they met some people out hunting. He sent them back to the camp to tell the people there to camp in a large circle and to put up his lodge in the center. He waited until he thought the camp was all arranged, and then went into it. The people in the village supposed that those who brought the word were mistaken about its being Sweet Medicine, but they said they were sure. When they reached the camp, all was arranged as he had ordered. He went to the lodge and hung the arrows in front of it, over the door.

In the morning the man unrolled his bundle and took four arrows from it. These were the four medicine-arrows. He said, "Here are four arrows for you to keep. Make your arrows to kill the buffaloes like these." Afterward he hung the bundle of arrows on the door of his brother's lodge. Then he moved about and lived with them and made arrows himself.

He lived with these people for four or five generations, four long, long lives. Young people would grow up, get old, and die; other young people would be born, grow up, get old, and die; but still this man lived. All through the summer he was young, like a young man. When fall came, and the grass began to dry up, he began to look older; and about the middle of the winter he was like a very old man and walked bent over and crooked. In spring he became young again. At last he died. This man got a certain wood, very hard, and taking a piece about a foot long, and twirling the point of it on a dry buffalo-chip, he could make fire. He then told them to take the leg-bone of the deer or antelope, and cut it off, and make a pipe of it. He gathered a certain weed, and told them to dry it, and to smoke it in their pipes.

These men, Sweet Medicine and his brother, lived with the people for a long time and taught them how to live, how to tan skins, to make clothing, and to dress robes.

At last Sweet Medicine said to the people, "I shall not be with you long now. I chose the wrong person; I wanted to be too good-looking. Now I am getting old and have lived as long as I want to; but before I die I have something to tell you. Now my people, you must not forget what I am telling you this day, and all the things I have told you and taught you. After I am dead, you must come together often and talk over all these things; and when you do so, always call my name. A time is coming when you will meet other people, and you will fight with them. You will kill each other. Each tribe will want the land of each other tribe, and you will be fighting always."

He pointed to the south and said, "Far away in that direction is another kind of buffalo, with long hair hanging down from its neck and a tail that drags on the ground. You will find it an animal with a round hoof, not split like a buffalo's, and with teeth in the upper part of its mouth, as well as below. This animal you shall ride on and pack."

"The buffalo will disappear; and when the buffalo have gone, the next animal you have to eat will be spotted. When you get toward the end, you people will begin to become gray very young and will come to marry even your relations. You may reach a point where you will be ashamed of nothing and will act as if you were crazy."

"You will soon find among you a people who have hair all over their faces, and whose skin is white. When that time comes, you will be controlled by them. The white people will be all over the land, and at last you will disappear".

Sweet Medicine died in the summer, when he was a young man. His brother also had lived with the people for a long time. He did not grow old and then young again. He continued to be a middle-aged man for many generations. At last he too died, having lived longer than Sweet Medicine.

18. YELLOWTOP-TO-HEAD WOMAN

(Cheyenne)

This is the story of the beginning of people, way up on the other side of the Missouri River. It is very level and sandy there.

There was a big camp, and they had nothing to eat. Everyone was hungry. All they had to depend on was the fish, geese, and ducks in the little lakes. Early one morning an old man went through the village calling out for two chiefs who must be fast runners. They were told to go around to all the small lakes and see if they could find anything to eat. They were told not to come back until they found something, for the camp was in great need of food. The children were starving.

These two men were to be trusted. They travelled far in different directions, and in four days came back without having found anything. The cry went round for every one to pack the dog travois, for they must move anyhow.

That night when they made camp, all the chiefs gathered in the center of the village and sent for two young men, the sons of chiefs, and the chiefs told them to go on ahead of the camp and not to return until they had found something. They said, "You must try hard. You can hear the old people and the children crying for something to eat, so be sure to find something. Do not come back until you do so."

After these boys set out, the elder said to the younger, "Now we must find something before we come back or the people will starve." So they started, going straight north. After they had been gone eight days, they saw in front of them a high peak, and just this side of it something that looked blue. One of them said, "I am nearly dead. I am afraid I can't travel much farther." The other said, "Do you see that peak over there? We will both go over there and die, and it will be a mark over us. It will be our burying-place." The peak was high and steep. The other said, "We will go there and die together." They walked toward it, and when they got near, they saw that between it and them ran a large stream. They sat down on the bank and looked across and saw that the peak came right down to the other bank. Off to one side of the peak ran a high bluff. The elder said, "Take off your leggings and let us cross over to the peak." He took the lead and they waded in. The water came up to mid-thigh, then higher. Finally, the one behind called out and said, "My friend, I cannot move. Something has hold of me. I cannot move. Tell my people what has happened to me. Tell them not to cry for me. Some mysterious power holds me." As the man stood fast, he called out, "My friend, come back and shake hands with me for the last time." The older boy turned back and approached his friend weeping and shook hands with him. Then he left him and the younger gave his warcry, and the elder went on, weeping, toward the peak. He came out of the water and walked up and down the bank, weeping.

Just then he saw a man come out of the peak and come towards him. This man had a large coyote skin around him, the head coming up over his head. He carried a large knife in his hand. The boy ran to him and said, "Something is holding my friend." The coyote man said, "Stand where you are!" and went on toward the boy in the water. Just before he reached him he dived down under the water and cut the big serpent that was holding the boy. He cut its head off with the knife he was carrying. The other saw the serpent rise up, after its head had been cut off, and splash water in every direction. The coyote man then came to the top of the water and called to the boy on the shore, "Go to the peak. There is a big rock there. That is the door. You will find an old woman there. Tell her that grandfather has killed the serpent he has been trying to get, and that she must bring some hide ropes."

When the boy reached the place, the rock flew open like a door, and an old, old woman came out. He said, "Grandfather has killed the serpent he has been trying to get for so long." The old woman said, "That is true, he has been trying to kill it for a long time." Then the boy went back to where the coyote man was standing. The coyote man said, "Go get your friend and bring him out of the water." When he reached him, the younger said, "I can walk no farther. I cannot move." So the elder turned his back to him and got him on his shoulders and carried him to the bank and laid him there. Then the coyote man said, "Let him lie there a while. Help me drag out this serpent." They both waded in again and cut the serpent to pieces and dragged it out with a rope. When they had brought it all to the bank, the coyote man said to the elder boy. "Lift your friend on your shoulders, and I will carry his feet, and we will take him up to the peak." Meanwhile the old woman was carrying up all the meat. The elder boy took his friend on his back, and the coyote man held up his feet, and they carried him up to the peak.

When he got close to the rock, the coyote man threw the door open and they went inside, and the boy saw that the peak was a lodge, a very fine lodge, and on one side they had a sweathouse. The coyote man told the elder boy to start a fire and to carry his friend into the sweathouse. He started a fire, and after the stones were heated, they put the younger boy in the sweathouse. When they got the stones inside, the coyote man sprinkled water on them four times. Meanwhile, the younger boy was beginning to become discolored where the serpent had caught hold of him. Four times they sprinkled water on the stones, and after they had done it the fourth time, they told him that he was cured, and he arose and walked out of the sweathouse. The old woman called to them to come and eat, for she knew that they were nearly starved. Standing by the fire were two jars in which she was cooking. She said, "I know you are very hungry." She had two white bowls made of stone. They were as white as snow. She put meat in each dish. She handed each of them a white flint knife to cut with and told them to eat all they wanted. After they had finished eating, the coyote man, who was sitting on one side of the lodge with the old woman, said, "Look over there!" They looked and saw a very handsome young woman sitting on the other side of the lodge. They looked at her, and the coyote man said, "Now, my grandsons, I want to ask you two things. Do you want to take that woman for your sister, or do you want to marry her?" The elder said, "My friend is poorer than I. Let him take her for his wife." The coyote man said, "Ha-ho, that is good. I am glad to hear that."

After the younger had chosen the woman for his wife, the coyote man told them to look to the north. They did so, and they saw a big field of corn. He told them to look to the east, and there they saw the country covered with buffalo. He told them to look to the south, and there were elk, deer, and all kinds of game. A little to one side of where the elk were, as they looked again, they saw herds of horses. To the west, they saw all kinds of birds. The coyote man said to them, "Now you shall go to your home. Take that woman back with you to your camp; it is very fortunate one of you selected her for his wife. She is to be a great helping power to your people. She will take everything I have shown you to your people. Everything will follow her." They went out of the lodge and stood looking toward the south --- the direction the two young men had come from. They stood in this order. The old woman on the east side, then the coyote man, then the young woman, then her husband, and then his friend.

Now for the first time the two young men knew that this woman was the daughter of these two old people, for the coyote man said, "My daughter, rest four times on your way." He meant make four stops, not four nights, for he had given her the power to travel fast. The coyote man said they would arrive at their village that night, and that the next morning they would see all these animals around their camp. He also told his daughter that if there was ever a little buffalo calf brought in not to say to it, "My poor animal." The old woman said, "If they ever bring in any kind of fowl, never, never say to it, "My poor animal. Do not express pity for any suffering creature." The coyote man said to her, "I send you there for a special purpose. These poor people have only fish and a few birds to eat, but now that you are there,

there will be plenty of game of all kinds. The skins of all these animals will also be useful for wearing."

The three young people started for home and rested four times, and as they started the fifth time, they passed the crest of a hill and saw the village below. When the people saw that there were three persons coming back instead of two, the whole village came running toward them. They came close and looked at the handsome woman. They spread down a robe and carried her in it to her father-in-law's lodge. He was one of the head chiefs. They all three sat together, and the elder boy was the spokesman. All crowded close about them to hear the news they had brought. He said, "Old men, women, and chiefs, societies of braves, and children, we have brought this woman down here from far up north. She has brought great power with her. You people are saved from hunger. Now when the sun goes down and comes up again, you will see many things around you." That night as they went to sleep they heard noises all around them.

Early the next morning an old man called out, "Get ready, get ready," and they saw the buffalo close to the village. The wind was blowing toward the east, and there was just a little open space in front of the village. The buffalo were all around. The Indians ran out with their bows and flint-headed arrows and killed many buffalo. The buffalo were so near that they shot them from their lodge doors. The elder boy told the people that they must kill only what they needed and that then they must leave the buffalo alone. The buffalo came right up to the lodge in which the woman lived and rubbed against it. She sat and laughed.

One of the chiefs went into the lodge where this woman lived and said to her father-in-law, "All the chiefs will come here in the morning to hold a council and arrange some plan, deciding what to do." This chief said, "We want to talk about returning favors to the girl and her people, because they have been kind to us and brought us these animals." The woman said nothing, but her father-in-law answered, "Come together here in the morning, and we will smoke and talk."

When morning came, all the chiefs gathered together and came to the lodge to talk with the woman. She was not like the other women. She would hardly ever speak. She did not even go out and look around as other women do, but always sat in the lodge. When the chiefs came in, each in turn thanked her for what she had done and what she had brought, and asked if they could do any favor for her or her father for all that she had done for them. She said her father had not told her to accept favors, and she must do only what her father had told her.

Four years after that, this woman's husband said to her, "Let us go back and visit your father and tell him what the chiefs told you, for they asked if they might do you some favor." She said again, "No, my father did not say I was to accept any favors." But after a while she also said, "You are anxious to go there with me, let us go." So her husband went to his friend and said they were planning to go to the peak again. The woman told her husband to tell his friend not to come to the lodge till late at night, and he came after the village had gone to sleep. The woman said, "Everything is arranged. We will start now." It was then late in the night. They walked outside the circle of lodges. There they stood and the woman said, "Shut your eyes." They did so, and when she spoke again and said to them, "Open your eyes," they were standing in front of the door of the peak.

The woman said, "Father, we have come back. Open the door." The stone moved back, and they went in. The coyote man and his wife got up and embraced all three. After they had eaten, the coyote man said to his daughter, "I did not expect you back, as I did not tell you to return, and I do not ask for any favors. After you have rested, return to your village." The coyote man also said, "None of you must return here again. The only favor I ask is that no one ever says 'Poor animal' in speaking of a bird or a beast. Do not disobey me in that." They all stepped out, and as before stood in front of the lodge. The three shut their eyes, and when they opened them they were standing in their own village. Before they started out, the coyote man asked if they used the skins of the animals to wear and to make their lodges of. And when they said, "Yes," he said it was good and that he was glad.

Four years after they returned, some boys were dragging a little buffalo calf into camp. They were abusing it by throwing dirt into its eyes. The woman went out and said, "My poor calf!" Then she said, "I forgot," and she went and lay down in her lodge. When her husband came in, he saw that she was sorrowful and said, "What is it, my wife?" She answered, "I have done what I was told not to do. I said 'My poor calf,' and my father told me not to." That day the buffalo disappeared, and there were no signs of them. The next morning the woman said to her husband, "Go and call your friend." So he came. She said to both of them, "I am going back. If you wish to come back with me, I am glad. But if I must leave you here, you will have a hard time." They both spoke and said, "We love you and will go with you. Let us go to the center of camp and have it announced that we are going where your father and mother live, so that all the village may know what becomes of us." So it was announced, and all the people came running to where they were. She said that she had disobeyed her father in spite of his many cautions, and that they must go away. When she said that the whole village began to cry. Her friend then stood up and said that he and her husband were going also. He told his father and mother and all his people not to sorrow over him. Her husband also stood up and said the same, and that now they must work for his wife's father and mother. After that they announced that they would start that evening for the peak. All their relations wept, because they were going to leave them forever. That night all three disappeared, and no one ever knew what became of them. The name of the woman was Yellowtop-to-Head, for she had light colored hair. The buffalo never came back till they were brought from the spring by the two young men. This happened long before that.

19. THE ORIGIN OF CORN

(Wabanaki)

A long time ago, when Indians were first made, one man lived alone, far, far from any others. He didn't have any fire and lived on roots, barks, and nuts. This Indian became very lonesome. He was tired of digging roots. He lost his appetite, and after a while just lay dreaming in the sunshine.

After he had been sleeping several days, he awoke and saw something standing near. At first, he was quite scared. But when it spoke, his heart became glad, for it was a beautiful woman with long light hair. She was not like any Indian. He wanted her to come to him, but when he asked her she refused him. When he tried to approach her, she seemed to go farther away. He sang to her of his loneliness and begged her not to leave him. At last she told him that if he would do just what she said, he would always have her with him. He promised her he would.

She led him to a spot where there was very dry grass. Then she told him to get two very dry sticks and to rub them together quickly. Soon a spark flew out and caught on the grass. Quick as an arrow the ground was completely burned over. Then the beautiful girl said, "When the sun sets, take me by the hair and drag me over the burned ground." The Indian didn't want to do this, but she told him that wherever he dragged her something like grass would spring up, and between the leaves he would be able to see her hair. When this happened, the seeds would be ready for him to use. He did what she asked, and to this day when the Indians see the silk on the cornstalks they know the girl has not forgotten them.

The two stories that follow are only slightly explanatory. Tale 20, Forgetting the Song, does account for the number of coyotes at Kosenakwi and for the number of locusts at Wempo, but it is mostly concerned with another one of Coyote's foolish excapades. Tale 21, which was widespread in various forms throughout the West, moralizes mildly on gambling. The stickgame was a popular betting device among the Western tribes. Basically, it is a guessing game, though it can be played in hundreds of different ways.

20. FORGETTING THE SONG

(Zuñi)

Long, long ago lived Coyote. Not far away at Wempo lived the locusts. They would climb up the piñon-tree, and there all day long they sang:

> Locust, locust, flute.
> Locust, locust, flute.
> They climb up the piñon-tree.
> Flute, flute.

Coyote said to his wife, "I am going hunting." His wife said, "Go hunting. Maybe you will kill a rabbit. When you come, we will eat." He went hunting. He went to various places, until he finally went to the place where the locusts were. He heard a sound. The locusts were singing,

> Locust, locust, flute.
> Locust, locust, flute.
> They climb up the piñon-tree.
> Flute, flute.

He stopped. He said, "What is that? What a pretty song to put the children asleep!" They sang again,

> Locust, locust, flute.
> Locust, locust, flute.
> They climb up the piñon-tree.
> Flute, flute.

Coyote looked up into the tree. There were the locusts. He said, "Grandmothers, grandfathers, are you playing?" The locusts said, "Yes." Coyote said, "May I play too?" --- "Yes." --- Coyote said, "How can I get up?" The locusts said, "Sit on that branch. When we sing, you must sing too." Coyote jumped on the branch. They sang,

> Locust, locust, flute.
> Locust, locust, flute.
> They climb up the piñon-tree.
> Flute, flute.

Then Coyote repeated the song ponderously on a lower scale.

At sunset Coyote said, "I must go home. I am going." The locusts answered, "Go!" Coyote said, "I will come again tomorrow." The locusts said, "Come!" At mid-day, the locusts went up into the piñon-tree and sang their song. Coyote came. The locusts said, "Grandfather, are you coming?" Coyote said, "Yes." The locusts said, "Jump on the branch, and we will sing." He jumped on the branch. They sang,

> Locust, locust, flute.
> Locust, locust, flute.
> They climb up the piñon-tree.
> Flute, flute.

The sun went down. Coyote said, "I must go home." He went home, and he tried to sing the song to put his children to sleep. He sang,

> Locust, locust....

The rest of the song he forgot. His wife said, "Did you get the song?" He said, "No, I forgot it." He kept on saying,

> Locust, locust....

The next morning Coyote returned to Wempo. He said to the locusts, "I don't want to stay all day with you, but I want to take the song to my house." They sang for him. He left them. On his way back he fell into a mole-hole. He lost his song. He went back again to the locusts. He said, "I fell into a mole-hole and I forgot my song. You must sing it to me again. So they sang,

> Locust, locust, flute.
> Locust, locust, flute.
> They climb up the piñon-tree.
> Flute, flute.

He went off. He stepped on a brittle branch, and he hurt his foot and forgot his song. So he went back again. He said, "I stepped on a brittle branch, and I hurt my foot and I forgot my song. You must sing it for me again." They did. He went off once more. On his way he stepped on a cactus-plant. He fell down and hurt his foot and forgot the song. He returned to the locusts and said, "I stepped on a cactus-plant and fell and hurt my foot and forgot the song. You must sing it for me again. They sang it again. He went off still another time. This time he fell in another mole-hole and lost his song. He started back to the locusts. They said,

"We have sung for him four times. Let's not sing it for him again!"
So they went into their holes. They took off their masks, filled
them with pebbles, and set them in the piñon-tree. They saw Coyote
approaching, and they went into their tree.

Coyote came and said to the locusts' masks, "Sing for me
again. I fell into a mole-hole, and I forgot the song." They did
not answer. Coyote said, "Sing to me, or I'll come up on the tree
and eat you." They did not answer. "I shall ask you four times,"
said Coyote. "Once, will you sing for me?" They did not answer.
"Twice, will you sing for me?" They did not answer. "Three
times, will you sing for me?" They did not answer. "I shall give
you one more chance. Will you sing the song you sang to me?"
Nobody answered. He said, "They want to be eaten up." He jumped
up and seized the masks. He knocked out his teeth as they closed
on the pebbles in the masks. His mouth was full of blood. He
went to his house. His wife said, "Why is your mouth full of
blood?" Coyote said, "I asked the locusts to sing me a song. I
asked them four times. Then I jumped at them and knocked my
teeth out on their masks." Coyote said, "We must not live here.
We must live where we can live all the time." So they went to
Kosenakwi. This is why at Kosenakwi you can always see coyotes,
just as at Wempo you always see locusts. Thus it was long ago.

21. THE CONQUERING GAMBLER

(Tahlatan)

A boy addicted to playing the stick game spent all his time
gambling. When he heard of an important game of a noted gambler,
he went there to play, even if it was far away. He was very successful and nearly always won. Thus he became wealthy, although
he was only a boy. His father was a wealthy man and possessed
many slaves. One night a strange man came to the village and
challenged the boy to play. He promptly accepted the challenge,
and the two went outside to play. The man won all the boy's goods.
The boy bet his father's slaves and lost ten of them. Then the
boy staked his mother against two of the slaves. He lost again.
He staked his father, his uncle, all his relatives, and finally all
the people of the village, and lost. The stranger took all he had
won and departed, leaving the boy all alone.

This man was Sea-Man. He took all the people to his house
under the sea. The boy had no one to gamble with and nothing
to bet. He wandered in and out of the houses, crying all the time.
One day he saw smoke issuing from a bunch of grass. He found

a house there, and a very small old woman inside. She was the small black mouse. She said, "Grandson, where are you going? What troubles you?" He answered, "I have gambled away everything I had, even my friends and all my people." She asked him if he was hungry, and he answered, "Yes." She put on a kettle and split a single fish egg with a wedge. She put half of it into the kettle to boil. When it was cooked, she put the food on a dish and placed it before the boy. He thought, "The food will not be enough." But when he ate it, he found he was satisfied. She told him to stay there that night and added, "You must arise early in the morning and wash just at daylight. Then go to that steep place over there. You will see something growing there. Pull it out by the roots and eat it." He did as directed and after eating went to the steep place where he saw a beautiful plant growing. He ate it and it made him sleepy. Next Mouse-Woman said, "Tomorrow morning bathe and go to the beach. There you will find something. The boy returned with a sea-otter skin. He had fasted two mornings and used no fire at night. Mouse-Woman said to him, "Golden-eyed Duck shall be your brother. When you play the stick game, never point or choose a stick until he directs you." He slept that night without fire, arose early, and continued to fast. As directed by Mouse-Woman, he went down to the edge of the sea and challenged Sea-Man to a game.

The water opened like a door, and Sea-Man came out of his house. When it opened, the boy could see his parents and all the people working in a big house as slaves. He had hidden his duck-brother on his person. Sea-Man had a trump-stick which was really a fish. When the boy pointed at it or chose it, it always jumped aside. This was the reason he had always lost when playing with Sea-Man. Duck noticed this and warned the boy, who bet his otter-skin against his father. Duck instructed the boy to point a number of times near the fish-stick, so as to tire the fish out. Then Duck told him to point quickly at the fish. The boy did this and won. Acting on Duck's advice, he won back his parents, relatives, and all the people and goods. They all came back to the village.

This is why plants are used as charms to obtain good luck in gambling and also why it is bad for young people to gamble too much.

Tales of trips to other worlds than this were popular among the Indians. Of these, Tale 22, the *Star Husband* was particularly well-known, being distributed all the way from New England to the Pacific. The stories assume two main forms: ones similar to that printed here from the Sekani of what is now British Columbia; and others involving a single girl and her star-son who returns to earth to undertake adventures not unlike those of Afterbirth Boy. In South America, there is a similar myth involving a man who wishes to marry a star-woman.

Journeys to the land of the dead were also common. Some of these tales involve an Orpheus motif, the hero going to the land in order to bring back a lost sweetheart or wife. Others, like the two printed here, do not possess this worldwide element.

The Aurora Borealis has been the subject of folktales in Western Europe and Asia, as well as in North America. Frequently, the phenomenon is associated with the souls of dead persons.

22. STAR HUSBAND

(Sekani)

There were two sisters who were playing in front of their house. They made a small hut and lay down in it to sleep. During the night they awoke and saw the stars in the sky. One of the sisters said, "Do you see that white star? I will have him for my husband. You take that red star." They joked and laughed about this and finally went to sleep again. While they were sleeping two men entered their hut. One of the men wore a white blanket, the other wore a red blanket. The latter married the elder sister, while the former took the younger for his wife. They removed them from the house into the sky. They were the two stars of whom the girls had been speaking. When the sisters awoke and saw the strange men by their sides, they did not know where they were.

On the following morning their mother called them to come to breakfast. When she did not receive an answer, she grew angry and went to call the girls. Then she saw that they had disappeared. During the night a boy had heard how the girls had been talking about the stars, and thus the people believed that the stars had abducted the girls. The stars go out every night with bow and arrows, hunting cariboos. Then they look through holes in the sky and see what is going on on earth.

The two stars who had married the girls also went out every night and brought home many cariboos. The young women skinned and carved them. They made gloves, shoes, and dresses from the skins. They cut long thongs from the skins of others, cutting spirally around their bodies. They hid the clothing and the thongs carefully from their husbands. There was no water, no cloud, and no rain in the sky, and they were always suffering thirst. They had nothing to eat but meat. Therefore they longed to return to their own country. When they had prepared enough thongs and cloths they made ready to escape. One day, when their husbands had started on a long hunting expedition, they went to a hole in the sky. They tied stones to one end of a thong and let it down towards the earth. When one thong was paid out, they tied a new thong to the end of the first, and thus they worked from morning until night. The one woman brought cloths and thongs from the hiding-place, while the other let them down. Finally, after four days, they felt the rope striking the ground. They could not see the earth because it was hidden by smoke. They shook the thong and it fell a little farther, but finally it seemed to have reached the ground. At least they felt it was held by something. Now they tied two pairs of sticks together, one being on each side of the rope. They put on four suits of clothing, four pairs of shoes, and four pairs of gloves. The elder sister stepped on one pair of sticks and began to glide down, the sticks acting as a brake. The rope swung to and fro, and the sister who had remained behind gradually lost sight of her. Finally, the young woman reached the end of the rope and found herself on top of a tall tree. Her clothing and her gloves were almost worn through by friction. Then she shook the rope, and upon this signal her sister began to slide down in the same manner. She came down very much quicker, because her sister was holding the end of the rope. Looking upward, she beheld a small dot in the air. It was coming nearer and increased in size. Soon she recognized her sister, who finally reached the top of the tree. There they were on the top of a tall spruce tree, and there was no way of getting down. They broke off some branches and made a bed in the tree. The elder sister, before starting, had tied an additional bit of thong about her waist, thinking that she might use it in case the long rope did not reach the ground. She untied it and fastened it to the long rope, but still it was not long enough.

After a while, the young woman saw a number of men passing the foot of the tree. They were armed with bows and arrows and were on snowshoes. They recognized Wolf, Bear, and many other animals. They called to them, asking them to help them down, but they passed without paying any attention. The next morning they saw another man approaching the tree. They recognized Fisher. They called to him and he at once climbed the tree. The young women asked him to carry them down, but he demanded that they first have intercourse with him. The elder one said, "I will, but first carry me down." Fisher finally agreed and carried her down. When they got to the foot of the tree, she demanded that he first carry down her youngest sister. Reluctantly, he agreed to do so. Then he demanded from the youngest sister that she sleep with him. She said, "I will, but carry me down first." He took her down. When he insisted on his wishes, the elder sister said, "We are almost starved; first bring us some food." He went away and soon returned, carrying a bear he had killed. During his absence, the young women had lighted a fire. He wanted to roast the bear meat, but they said they wanted to eat it boiled. Fisher made a basket of bark, and placed stones into the fire, which he intended to use to boil water in the basket. Meanwhile the women had hidden a few pieces of meat under their blankets, and now they pretended to go to fetch water in which to boil the meat. As soon as they were out of sight they ran away down the mountains. After a while, the elder sister flung a piece of meat at a tree, asking it to whistle. They went on, and again she threw a piece of meat at a tree, asking it to talk. In this manner she continued to give meat to all the trees.

When the young women did not return, Fisher followed them to a brook, where they had gone to fetch water. He discovered their tracks and saw that they had escaped. He pursued them. Soon he came to the tree which they had asked to whistle. It did so when Fisher went past. Then he thought they were on the tree, climbed it, and searched for them. When he did not find them, he continued his pursuit. He came to the second tree, which spoke when he went past. Again he thought the women might be on the tree. He climbed up, but did not find them. Thus he lost so much time that they were able to escape.

Towards evening they reached a deep canyon. They walked along its edge, and soon they were discovered by Grizzly Bear, who was living there. He wanted to sleep with them, and they did not dare to refuse. But they said, "First go bring us something to eat. We are almost starving." While Bear was away hunting, the girls built a platform over the steep precipice of the canyon. It overhung the abyss and was held in place by two ropes which were tied to a tree that grew near the edges of the canyon. Its outer edge was supported by two slanting poles which leaned against a ledge a short distance down the precipice. When the bear came back, he found them apparently asleep on this platform. He did not bring any meat; he had only roots and berries. The young women said that they could not eat that kind of food and demanded that he go hunting again. It had grown dark, however, and Bear said he would go out the next morning. They lay down on the platform, and the young women induced Bear to lie near the edge, while they lay down near the tree to which the platform was tied. They kept away from Bear, promising to sleep with him after he had obtained food for them. Early in the morning, when Bear was asleep, they arose without disturbing him, cut the ties with which the platform was fastened to the tree, and tipped it over, throwing Bear into the canyon.

The women travelled on, and for a whole month they did not meet with a soul. Then one day they discovered tracks of snowshoes, and soon they found the hut of a woman who had given birth to a child. They entered, and recognized one of their friends. They stayed with her for a short time, and when the young mother was ready to return to the village, they sent her on in order to tell their relatives of their return. She went to the mother of the lost girls, and told her they were waiting in the woods, but she would not believe the news. The young mother returned to her friends and told them that their mother would not believe that they had come back. Then they gave her as a token a skin hat that was decorated with stars. She took it to the village and showed it to the mother of the two young women. Then she began to think that there might be some truth in the report, and went out to look. There she saw and recognized her daughters. At that time all the men were out hunting. The women on hearing of the return of the two lost girls went out to see them, and they told of their adventures. Then they climbed two trees, tied their skin belts to the branches, and hanged themselves.

23. NORTHERN LIGHTS

(Wabanaki)

Old Chief Morning Star had an only son, who was different from the other boys. He worried the old chief. He would not stay and play with the others, but would take his bow and arrows and leave home for days at a time, always going towards the North. When he came home, they would say, "Where have you been, what have you seen?" But he would say nothing. At last the old chief said to his wife, "The boy must be watched. I will follow him."

So the next time Morning Star kept in his son's path and travelled for a long time. Suddenly his eyes closed and he could not hear. He had a curious feeling. Then he knew nothing. After a while he opened his eyes in a queer land of light. There was no sun, no moon, no stars, just a country lighted by this peculiar glow. He saw many beings, but they were all different from his people. They gathered around him and tried to talk, but he could not understand their language. Morning Star didn't know where to go or what to do. He was well treated by this strange tribe. He watched their games and was attracted to a wonderful game of ball he had never seen before. It seemed to turn the light to many colors, and the players all had lights on their heads. All also wore a curious kind of belt called a Rainbow belt.

In a few days an old man came to speak to Morning Star in his own language and asked him if he knew where he was. The old chief said, "No." Then the old man said, "You are in the country of the Northern Lights. I came here many years ago. I was the only one from the lower country, but now there is a boy who comes to visit us every few days." Then Morning Star asked the old man how he got there, what way he came. The old man said, "I follow a path called the Spirit's Path, the Milky Way." --- "This must be the same path I came," said the old chief. "Did you have a queer feeling as if you lost all knowledge when you travelled?" --- "Yes," said the old man, "I couldn't see or hear." --- Then Morning Star said, "We did come by the same path. Can you tell me how I can get home?" --- "Yes, the Chief of the Northern Lights will send you home safe." --- "Well, can you tell me where I can see my son?" --- Then the old man told Morning Star, "You will see him playing ball if you watch." Morning Star was very glad to hear this, and soon the old man went around the wigwams telling all to go and have a game of ball. Morning Star was to go too.

When the game began he saw many beautiful colors in the playground. The old man asked him, "Do you see your boy there?" The old chief said he did, "The one with the brightest light on his head is my son." Then they went to the Chief of the Northern Lights, and the old man said, "The Chief of the Lower Country wants to go home, and he also wants his boy." So the Chief of the Northern Lights called his people together to say good-bye to Morning Star and his son. Then he ordered two great birds to carry them home. When they were travelling the Milky Way, the old chief felt the same strange way he had when they were going. When he came to his senses, he found himself near home. His wife was very glad he had returned. She was afraid Morning Star was lost.

24. THE LAND OF THE DEAD

(Coos)

An Indian who lived in a certain village suddenly became ill. He had three sons and said to them, "If I should die, let me lie five days before you bury me." Soon he died, and his sons kept the body in the house over night. On the next morning they put him outside, at a distance from the house. They laid him on a board, put a couple of boards on each side edgewise and one on top, and although they watched him they did not see that he had gone, because his body remained there.

His soul, however, went away. As soon as he started, he

lost his way and did not know where to go. Finally he came to a
wide trail. He saw fresh tracks on the trail and alongside of it.
So he followed these tracks. Sticks were lying across the trail,
marked with red paint by people who had touched them. Soon he
came to the top of the trail, and when he began to go on a downhill grade he heard sea-gulls and eagles making a noise. He
wondered where those birds could be, because he could not see
them. Then he came to a village. When the people from the village saw him, they began to shout from the other side, "A man
is coming down, a man is coming down!" And they all ran to
their canoes and went to fetch him. But he went to the landing-
place and stood there smiling, because some of them had just pieces
of canoes, others only half-canoes, and the rest of the canoes had
holes punched in one end. When the people came nearer, he saw
among them his father, his eldest brother, and many other people
he knew. But they did not land. They only looked at him from
the river and said, "You are a *stöndi*." And his father said to
him, "Your grandmother is living down the river. Go there." So
he went to the place where his grandmother was, and when he came
there he saw his grandfather sitting by the door and whittling a
small stick, while his grandmother was sitting just inside the door,
making a small basket. He greeted them, and they all went into
the house. The house was very clean and nice. In one corner
of the room there was a small basket hanging from the wall. The
old man soon built a fire, took this basket down, put his hands into
it three times, and took out a small dish. Then he put the little
basket back and placed the dish in front of his grandson, who at
first could not see anything in it. But when he looked again, it
was full of lice. He became scared and threw the dish into the
fire, and the old man said to him, "Oh, my grandson, people always eat lice when they come here first." His grandparents knew
all the time that he was a *stöndi*, but they did not tell him. They
told him, however, that a woman had arrived the day before, and
that they were going to dance for her, and play shinny, cards, and
many other games, after the dance. After a while the man looked
through the window and saw a fish-trap built clean across the river,
and he thought to himself, "I am going to cross the river on the
dam this evening." But his grandparents told him not to go down
to the river, because something might get hold of him and devour
him. He obeyed them and stayed in the house. But the next morning he said to himself, "I will go down and take a swim. I wonder
why they did not want me to go down to the river." So he left
the house and began to wade out into the river. Soon eels began

to stick to his legs and hung fast. But they did not bother him, and he kept on swimming. After he was through swimming he took two of the largest eels to the house. His grandparents were sitting by the fire. When he came in, he placed the eels near them. But the old couple became scared. The old woman crawled away on her hands and knees to the end of the house, and the old man hid himself in a corner. In the meantime the young man whittled a small stick and roasted the eels on it. When they were about to be done, they began to smell very nice, and the old couple came out from their corners and shared in the meal.

In the evening, after the old people had gone to bed, the young man crossed the river on the fish-weir and came to the dance house. He looked in and saw a woman that he knew. She was standing in the middle of the room, and people were dancing around her in a circle. Everyone who went by touched her on the top of her head. Soon the dancers noticed him, and they began to shout, "Do you see that *stöndi* outdoors looking into the house?" The young man ran away and went back to his grandparents, who said to him, "Whenever anybody comes here and eats lice he becomes a resident of this village and cannot go back anymore. You are still a live person and able to go back." But he did not want to go back yet, because he wanted to take another good look at the dance. So when night came, he crossed the river again and went to the dance-house. There the same woman was distributing presents which had been put in her grave when she was buried, saying, "Your brother sends you this; your father sent you this; your mother sends you this." When the people in the house saw him, they said, "That *stöndi* is looking in again. Do you see him?" So he went back to his grandparents and said, "My children are waiting for me, and I have to go back." And about eight o'clock he started on his way home.

In the meantime his body, which was lying near the house covered up with boards, was getting rotten. His mouth came out of shape, and his flesh was beginning to look like a sponge. Near noontime on the fifth day, his corpse began to squeak and crack. It squeaked four times, and his sons took away the boards carefully. When it squeaked the fifth time, the body seemed to move. Then his children took off all covers from him, except a single blanket. As soon as this was done, his body stopped squeaking. Suddenly he began to move his arms and legs under the blanket, and soon he stretched his feet. His oldest son was watching him all the time. He made a blazing fire by his side. The dead men threw off his blanket and sat up. His long hair was hanging down in front of him and reached way to his waist. His son said to him, "My father, I am watching you. I have been watching you all the time." To this he replied something that the boy could not understand. And the boy said to him, "My father, I do not know what you said." So he said to his son, "I have some lunch here in a little basket. You may eat it. Your grandmother sends it to you." But the boy could not see the basket at all and shouted to his brothers, "Come here, our father has come back!" They all hurried up and came to see their father. They wanted to warm some water and bathe him in it, but he said, "I am not going to take a bath, my children. I got back all right." His eyes appeared to be swelled, as if he had been asleep for a long time. When he arose from the ground, he said to his sons, "You need not eat the lunch I brought now. You can look for it in the water tomorrow. I have in it one cooked and one fresh flounder." On the next morning the boys found many flounders in the river, some half cooked, and others half fresh, swimming about in the water. And this man never grew old, but always remained a young man. Only his children were getting old, very, very old.

When the Journal of American Folklore began its "Good Story" section in 1943, Water Jar Boy was the first tale selected. This text is clearly fragmentary, however, as further adventures should ensue. Tales featuring a hero who springs from a jug, who has a brief childhood, and who goes on to adventures like those of Bloodclot and Afterbirth Boy were common enough to the California and Southwestern Indians.

25. WATER JAR BOY

(Tewa)

The people were living at Sikyatki. There was a fine look-ing girl who refused to get married. Her mother made water jars all the time. One day as she was using her foot to mix some clay, she told her daughter to go on with this while she went for water. The girl tried to mix the clay on a flat stone by stepping on it. Somehow some of it entered her. This made her pregnant, and after a time she gave birth. The mother was angry about this, but when she looked she saw it was not a baby that had been born, but a little jar. When the mother asked where it came from the girl just cried. Then the father came in. He said he was very glad his daughter had a baby. When he found out that it was a water jar, he became very fond of it.

He watched it and saw it move. It grew, and in twenty days it had become big. It could go about with the other children and was able to talk. The children also became fond of it. They found out from his talk that he was Water Jar Boy. His mother cried, because he had no legs or arms or eyes. But they were able to feed him through the jar mouth.

When snow came the boy begged his grandfather to take him along with the men to hunt rabbits. "My poor grandson, you can't hunt rabbits; you have no arms or legs."

"Take me anyway," said the boy. "You are so old, you can't kill anything." His grandfather took him down under the mesa where he rolled along. Pretty soon he saw a rabbit track and followed it. Then a rabbit ran out, and he began to chase it. He hit himself against a rock. The jar broke, and up jumped a boy.

He was very glad his skin had been broken and that he was a big boy. He had lots of beads around his neck, earstrings of turquoise, a dance kilt and moccasins, and a buckskin shirt. He was fine-looking and handsomely dressed. He killed four jack-rabbits before sunset, because he was a good runner.

His grandfather was waiting for him at the foot of the mesa, but did not know him. He asked the fine looking boy, "Did you see my grandson anywhere?"

"No, I did not see him."

"That's too bad; he's late."

"I didn't see anyone anywhere," said the boy. Then he said, "I am your grandson." He said this because his grandfather looked so disappointed.

"No, you are not my grandson."

"Yes, I am."

"You are only teasing me. My grandson is a round jar and has no arms and legs."

Then the boy said, "I am telling you the truth. I am your grandson. This morning you carried me down here. I looked for rabbits and chased one, just rolling along. Pretty soon I hit myself on a rock. My skin was broken, and I came out of it. I am the very one who is your grandson. You must believe me." Then the old man believed him, and they went home together.

When the grandfather came to the house with a fine looking man, the girl was ashamed, thinking the man was a suitor. The old man said, "This is Water Jar Boy, my grandson. The grandmother then asked how the water jar became a boy, and the two men told her. Finally, the women were convinced.

The boy went about with the other boys of the village. One day he said to his mother, "Who is my father?"

"I don't know," she replied. He kept on asking, but it just made her cry. Finally he said, "I am going to find my father, tomorrow."

"You can't find him. I have never been with any man so there is no place for you to look for a father," she said.

"But I know I have one," the boy said. "I know where he lives. I am going to see him."

The mother begged him not to go, but he insisted. The next day she fixed food for him, and he went off toward the southwest to a place called Horse Mesa Point. There was a spring at this place. As he approached he saw a man walking a little way from the spring. He said to the boy, "Where are you going?"

"To the spring," the boy answered.

"Why are you going there?"

"I want to see my father."

"Who is your father?"

"He lives in this spring."

"Well, you will never find your father," said the man.

"Well, I want to go to the spring. My father is living in it." said the boy.

"Who is your father?" asked the man again.

"Well, I think you are my father."

"How do you know that?"

"I just know, that's all."

Then the man stared hard at the boy, trying to scare him. The boy just kept on saying, "You are my father." At last the man said, "Yes, I am your father. I came out of the spring to meet you." He put his arms around the boy's neck. He was very glad his boy had come, and he took him down to the spring.

There were many people living there. The women and the girls ran up to the boy and put their arms around him, because they were glad he had come. This way he found his father and his father's relatives. He stayed there one night. The next day he went to his own home and told his mother he had found his father.

Soon his mother got sick and died. The boy thought to himself, "It's no use for me to stay with these people," so he went to the spring. There he found his mother among the other women. He learned that his father was Red Water Snake. He told his boy that he could not live over at Sikyatki, so he had made the boy's mother sick so she would die and come to live with him. After that they all lived together.

The most common form that the destruction of the world takes in primitive mythologies is the flood. However, great blizzards, droughts, and fires may wipe out man before his renewal. If a conflagration occurs in Indian myth, it may be the result of a forest fire set by the trickster, or it may be because of someone's tampering with the sun. One of these latter tales is similar to the Greek story of Phaeton, but more common is the account of the man who is angered by the sun and traps him. This story is popular across the Continent, and involves the efforts of a series of animals to rescue the world by cutting the Sun free. The Sun, who has been caught by a snare made of the pubic hair of the trickster's sister (a fact not clear in the tale below), is finally released by the mouse.

26. THE SUN-SNARE

(Tête de Boule)

Tcikabis was very fond of climbing trees. He had a magic power of making trees grow. He used to blow on the tree when he had reached the top, and the tree would increase its original length. Tcikabis would then climb to the new top and repeat the process. He thus was able to climb very high.

One time when he climbed much higher than usual, he came to a straight wide path which crossed the sky. "Who can it be who has such a fine wide path?" thought Tcikabis to himself. He decided to find out who it was that used this path, so he stretched himself across it and went to sleep. Pretty soon he was awakened by someone coming along the path. "Now I will find out who passes along here," thought Tcikabis. He looked up and saw the sun approaching. "Get out of my path," ordered the sun. "Go around me," replied Tcikabis, remaining where he was. "I cannot leave my path," said the sun. "You must get out of my way." But Tcikabis was not frightened by the sun. "Jump over me," he laughed. When the sun realized it was pointless to argue with Tcikabis, he stepped over him and proceeded on his way.

When the sun stepped over him, Tcikabis nearly died of the heat. When he looked up, he found all his clothes burned. In fact, he was severely scorched himself. Tcikabis was very angry at the sun for burning up his clothes. He then descended back to earth. His sister saw him coming and noticed that his clothes were nearly all burned off. "How did you burn your clothes, Tcikabis?" she asked. Tcikabis then told her. He decided to play a trick on the sun to even things up for his loss of clothes, for he was very angry. He then made a snare. "What are you going to do with the snare, Tcikabis?" asked his sister. He replied, "I am going to get even with the sun; he burned up my clothes yesterday." His sister tried to warn him against the trick, but he was not afraid.

Climbing back up the tree to the path, Tcikabis set the snare and waited at one side. Soon the sun came along on his daily journey and was caught in the snare. Immediately, everywhere there was darkness.

The darkness continued for some time. Finally Tcikabis realized that it would be dark always until the sun was set free. He then wanted to set the sun free, but he could not get close to the sun without being burned. He knew just how much damage the heat of the sun could do.

105

Tcikabis then collected all the small animals together and sent them, one after the other to release the sun. One by one they were killed. The heat of the sun was too great for them. Finally, mouse managed to free the sun from the snare. He chewed it with his teeth. The sun then continued on his journey, and right away there was light again.

Because sex involves the perpetuation of life, it has always been a central theme in the tales of man. In Tale 1, The Emergence, we saw the motif of the separation and the realization on the part of man that sex is a necessary part of existence. Tale 27, The Lecherous Father and His Daughter, like many of the amorous adventures of Coyote seems to indicate the improper way of participating in the reproductive process. The Tale, which was immensely popular with the Plains tribes, also explains the way in which Coyote became a wolf. Tale 28, The Toothed Vagina story, is most frequently a portion of the hero tale, The Sun Tests his Son-in-Law, but it also occurs in many trickster cycles as a separate incident. Here it is used by the Yurok as a means of explaining the origin of intercourse. The earlier Coyote incident, to which it is attached, involves the tabu against having intercourse before hunting that many tribes believed in.

27. THE LECHEROUS FATHER AND HIS DAUGHTER

(Southern Ute)

Suna'wavi had two daughters and a son. One day he was lying down in a little brush lodge. It was raining and the roof leaked so he asked his daughters to fix it. While they were doing this he looked up, getting a view of his eldest daughter that he had not had before. He began to lust for her. He thought of possessing both his daughters and consider how he might do so. He went out to hunt rabbits. He found an old rabbit bone and stuck it up in front of his tipi. There was snow on the ground and in cleaning it from his feet he purposely stepped on the bone. He cried out and his family came out. His wife pulled out the bone, but he pretended to be sick. He continued ailing for a long time; at last he said he was about to die. He told his family that after his death they should move far away to a big village. When they were there, some visitors were going to come from another part of the country. One was going to ride a gray horse, and he was the one his elder daughter should marry. There would be a lot of gambling there. This visitor would stand there. He would be good-looking, have his hair wrapped in otterskin and carry an otterskin quiver. "He is a good fellow, and if my daughter marries him she will never starve." He pretended to get worse. "When I die, I want you to burn me up. Roll me up in blankets on a pile of wood and burn me. Don't look back. If anyone looks back, someone else will die, it will bring bad luck." So they tried to burn him and went off without turning back. However, the little boy turned back and said, "My father rolled off." The old woman said, "Your father told you not to look back." --- "My father rolled off." --- "Well, then he is dead."

They went to the next village and told the people about the death; they were very sad. After several days visitors came from different parts of the country, and they looked for a man riding a gray horse, but he did not come, until one day they saw him. "That is the young man your father told us about. When he gets to those lodges, we'll tell him we want him." He stopped in the camp and stood behind the gamblers. He was carrying an otterskin quiver and his hair was decorated with otterskin. The little boy went up to him and ran back to tell his mother it was the man his father had spoken of. Then he was sent again to invite him to become the old woman's son-in-law. The boy called him, but the man replied, "Wait till sundown." The boy returned with the message. Suna'wavi spoke to the sun and made him set soon. He went to his family, who were seated, and sat between his daughters, who did not recognize him. The little boy, however, nudged his mother, saying, "He looks like father." His mother pushed him. "Don't say that, he is dead." But the boy repeated, "His face looks like father's." The old woman was ashamed to look and went to bed. "Take whichever girl you want." He chose the elder daughter. They went to bed. In the night the girl began to scream. The old woman said, "What's the matter? When I was young, it was the same way. Later it doesn't hurt."

The next morning the old woman asked the man to go where her husband had been in the habit of catching rats. He went off with the little boy. When they got to a big rat's house, the boy teased them out of their holes with a stick, while the man turned small, entered the holes, ate up the big ones inside and threw out the little ones. The boy said, "I think it is my father; this is the way he used to do." So he looked sharply and caught sight of four marks on Suna'wavi's teeth. Thus he recognized his father. He pushed his stick into the hole and rushed home. Suna'wavi said, "Go on teasing rats. What's the matter?" There was no answer; he saw the boy running off.

When near home the boy shouted, "That husband of yours is your father!" The people were scared. The old woman asked her daughter what her husband had done while they embraced. "It's your father, all right; that's what he does to me." She was furious and cut up his quiver and bows and arrows and threw them in the fire. Then she said, "Let us run away." They fled, going up toward the sky. Suna'wavi came home and said, "Wait for me." His wife answered, "You are no good; you did a dirty thing. We will not live with you anymore. We are going to the sky." --- "Wait for me." --- "No, it is too late. You are going to be turned into a wolf. At sundown you will go around the country and cry biting your tail." Suna'wavi said, "You shall be stars." --- "Yes, it is well." So they became the four stars that you can see in the evening.

28. THE TOOTHED VAGINA

(Yurok)

Coyote was a young man. He came out and saw two girls picking hazel nuts. They had a sweetheart, Cottontail Rabbit. Coyote came along and asked, "Where are you going?" They said, "We are going to camp out." Then Coyote said, "Can I go with you?" "Sure," they said, so he went with them.

They said to him," "We're going to camp right here on this sandbar," so they lay down and slept. Coyote slept in the middle between the girls, while Rabbit slept crossways at the foot. The blanket was narrow. Everytime they pulled it, they tore it in the middle, and Coyote pushed with his elbows and said, "Don't get so close to me, your breasts are too big. Don't get so close to me, I am going hunting tomorrow." Then he went to sleep and snored. The girls did not like him. They felt sorry for Rabbit sleeping at the foot, and they said, "Let's run away from Coyote." Rabbit said "All right," and they put logs on both sides of Coyote so he would think they were still there and went across the river and stayed. About noon they saw Coyote come out across the river. He· said to Rabbit, "Take me across." Rabbit would not do this, so Coyote got angry. He picked up rocks; he was going to fight that Rabbit. He swam across carrying the rocks. Rabbit got frightened. He made medicine to cause the river to be rough, so that Coyote would not be able to land. Soon Coyote drowned, and Rabbit thought he had two wives now and would never see Coyote again, because he was drowned.

Coyote landed way down the river, nothing but bones. Some girls thought they saw some nice wood in the river. They thought they would go and chop it. When they hit him, Coyote got up and said, "I was just sleeping right there," and went along up the river. He came across a camp where he saw many children. He thought, "I'll bet those are Rabbit's children." So he frightened all those children and made them go to sleep. Then he set fire to the camp and all the children were burned and he ran away up the river.

He had heard that there was a woman up the river who had killed many men. Every man who slept with her she killed. There was nothing but bones outside, and nobody ever passed that way anymore. He knew how she killed them: when a man had intercourse with her, she killed him. There were teeth inside her. Coyote decided to go up to see her. So he made sticks. He took those sticks and went up there and thought he was going to kill her.

He stood around near her house. Soon she came out. "Ah, come on," she said. She wanted him to sleep with her right away. Coyote thought everything was all right, so when that woman wanted him to have intercourse with her, he took one of the sticks and did what she wanted. Soon he felt the stick was wearing out, and he put another in its place. He had ten sticks. The woman kept talking about it. She said, "I'm glad, my husband." He changed sticks five times. After that she quieted down. At about the

eighth time she was saying something only once in awhile.   The
tenth time he killed her.   Coyote blew his breath and said, "Those
Indians are going to have a good time with women from now on.
They aren't going to be killed."

Part 3

THE EXCITEMENT OF LIVING

The motif of the rolling head is world-wide, being known to Europeans, Indonesians, and Africans, as well as to the North American Indians. The two tales printed here are quite representative of the Indian forms, although the Senecas told stories of flying skulls. Tale 30, in which the rock is usually irritated by being urinated on, makes a good companion piece to the more elaborate Tale 29, which is the classic form of the tale as known to the North Pacific and Plateau tribes. Sometimes this latter version stops with the man's feeding the snake's genitals to the woman, but usually it continues into the pursuit. The final portion of Tale 29 as printed here is really a separate story, which tells of the girl who can kill game by merely looking at it. It commonly attaches itself to the snake-lover, rolling head narrative. As the reader will note, the girl never uses her red quills. Evidentally, the informant forgot this repetitious portion.

29. ROLLING SKULL

(Cheyenne)

Once there was a lonely lodge where a man, his wife, and two children were living. One child was a girl, the other was a boy. In front of the lodge was a great lake and a trail leading from the lodge down to the shore. They used this trail to go for water. Everyday the man used to go hunting, but before starting he would paint his wife red all over — her face, her arms her whole body. At night, when he returned, he would always find her clean, the paint all washed off. When he started out to hunt, she would go for water, leaving the children alone in the lodge. When she returned with the water, the paint would be all gone and her hair unbraided. She always managed to get back with her water just before her husband arrived. He never brought in any meat.

Her husband thought it strange that every day the paint that he had put on his wife in the morning had disappeared, but he asked questions. One day he said to his daughter, "What does your mother do every day? When I leave I paint her; when I come back, she has no paint on." The girl answered, "Whenever you start out hunting, she goes for water; she is usually gone a long time."

The next day, the man painted his wife as usual. Then he took bow and arrows and went out of the lodge. But instead of going off in the direction he usually took to hunt, he went around down to the shore of the lake and dug a hole in the sand and buried himself there, leaving a little place where he could look out. He was going to watch.

The man had not been hidden long when he saw his wife coming carrying a bucket. When she got near the water's edge, she slipped off her dress and unbraided her hair. Then she walked close to the water, saying, "I am here." Soon the water began to move and a snake rose from the surface and crawled out on the land. The snake crept up to the woman. It wrapped itself about her body, began to have intercourse with her, and licked off all the red paint that was on her. When the man saw this happening, he rose from his hiding-place, rushed toward the embracing pair, and cut the monster to pieces with his knife. The pieces of the snake crept and rolled back into the lake. They were never seen again. Then, the man cut off the woman's head, cut off her arms at the elbow, her legs at the knee, and threw all the pieces into the water, saying, "Take your wife!" After that he opened the

117

body and took out a side of her ribs. He skinned the side of the ribs and returned to his lodge.

When he reached the lodge, he said, "Ah, my little children, I have had good luck. I have killed an antelope and have brought back some meat. Where is your mother?" The children replied, "Our mother has gone to bring water." --- "Well," he said, "since I killed my meat sooner than I thought, I brought it back to camp. Your mother will be here pretty soon. In the meantime, I'll cook something for you to eat. Then, I'll go out again." He cooked a kettle of meat and took it out to the children. The boy and the girl ate. The boy said to his sister, "Sister, this tastes like mother." He was the younger and was the last one who had suckled. "Oh," said his sister, "keep still. This is antelope meat." After the children had finished, the girl saved some meat for her mother to eat when she returned. The father got his moccasins and other things together and started off, intending never to come back. He was going to look for the tribe.

After he had gone, the children were sitting in the lodge. The girl was making moccasins and putting porcupine quills on them. As they sat there, they heard someone outside say, "I love my children, but they do not love me. They have eaten me." The girl said to her brother, "Look out of the door and see who's coming." The boy looked out and then cried, "Sister, here comes our mother's head." "Shut the door!" said the girl. The boy did. The girl then picked up her moccasins, her red, white, and yellow quills, and rolled them up. She also grabbed her root digger. In the meantime, the head rolled against the door and called out, "Daughter, open the door." The head would strike the door, roll partway up the lodge, and then fall back again.

The girl and her brother ran to the door, pushed it open, and stood to one side. The head rolled into the lodge and clear across to the back. The girl and boy sprang outside. The girl closed the door, and they ran away as fast as they could. As they ran, they heard their mother in the lodge calling to them. They ran and they ran. At last, the boy called out to his sister, "Sister, I am tired. I can't run any longer." The girl then took his robe and carried it for him. They ran on. At last, as they reached the top of the divide, they looked back. There they could see the head come rolling along over the prairie. Somehow it had gotten out of the lodge. The children kept running, but soon the head had almost overtaken them. The little boy was frightened and tired out.

The girl said, "This running is almost killing my brother. When I was a little girl playing, sometimes the prickly pears were so thick on the ground that I couldn't get through them." As she said this, she scattered a handful of the yellow porcupine quills on the ground. At once there was a great bed of prickly pears behind her. The pears were high and covered with great yellow thorns. The bed reached out for a long way in both directions.

When the head reached this place, it rolled up on the prickly pears and tried to roll over them. But it kept getting caught in the thorns and could not get through. It kept trying and trying for a long time, and finally it did get loose from the thorns and passed over. By this time, the boy and girl had gone a long way.

After they had gone a long way, they looked back and again saw the head coming. Somehow it had gotten through. When the boy saw the head coming, it frightened him so that he almost fainted. He kept calling out, "Sister, I am tired out. I can't run any longer." When the girl heard him say this, she said, "When I was a little girl, I often used to find the bullberry bushes very thick." As she said this, she threw a handful of the white quills behind her. Where they hit the ground, a great grove of thick thorny bullberry bushes grew up. This blocked the way, and the head stopped there for a long time.

The children ran on and on, toward the place where the people had last camped. But after awhile, when they looked back, they saw the head coming again. The boy called out, "Sister, I am tired out. I can't run any longer." Then the girl said, "When I was a little girl playing, I often came to ravines I could not cross." She stopped and drew the point of her root digger over the ground in front of her. She made a little groove in the ground. Then she placed the root digger across this groove, and she and her brother walked over on the root digger. When they had crossed over, the furrow became wider and wider and deeper and deeper until it was a great chasm. At the bottom, they could see a little water trickling. "Now," said the girl, "we will run no longer." --- "No, no," said the boy, "let's run." --- "No," said the girl, "I will kill our mother here."

Soon the head came rolling up to the edge of the ravine. It stopped there and said, "Daughter, where did you cross? Put your root digger on the ground so I can cross too." The girl tried to do this, but every time she tried the boy pulled her back. At last, she got the root digger down, and the head began to roll over the ravine. However, when it was about halfway across, the girl tipped the root digger, and the head fell in. The ravine closed on it.

After this, the children started on again to look for the people, and at last they found the camp and drew close to it. Before they had reached it, they could hear a man haranguing the camp. As they came nearer, they saw that it was their father. He was walking about the camp, calling out and saying that while he was out hunting his two children had killed and eaten their mother and that if the children came to the camp they ought to be kept from entering it. When they heard this, the children were scared. But they went into the camp anyway. When they entered, the people caught them and tied their hands and feet. The next day they moved away and left the children there, tied.

In the camp there was an old dog, who knew what had happened and so took pity on these children. That night the dog went into a lodge, stole some sinew and a knife and an awl, and took them into a hole where she had her pups. The next day, after all the people had gone, the children heard a dog howling, and soon they saw an old dog coming. She came over to them and said, "Grandchildren, I have come to take pity on you." The girl said, "Untie me first, and I can untie my brother." So the old dog began to gnaw at the rawhide strings with which the girl's hands were tied. The dog had no teeth and could not cut the cords, but she got them all wet and they began to slip. The girl kept working her hands and at last was free. She untied her legs and then went and untied her brother. That evening they went about through the camp, picking up old moccasins to wear. Both children were crying, and the dog was crying too. They sat on a hill near the camp, crying because they had nothing to eat and no place to sleep in. Winter was coming on, and they had nothing to cover themselves with. They sat there crying with their heads hanging down. However, the boy was looking about. All of a sudden he said to his sister, "Sister, look at that wolf; it is coming right towards us." --- "No," said the girl, "It is useless for me to look; I could not kill him by looking at him. We could not get him to eat." --- "But look, Sister," insisted the boy. "He is coming right up to us." At last, the girl looked, and when she looked the wolf fell down dead. Then the dog brought the things she had stolen and with the knife they cut up the wolf. From its skin they made a bed for the dog.

The children stayed in this camp, living well now, while the people in the main camp were starving. The children kept a big fire day and night, and used big logs so that it didn't go out at all.

After they had eaten the wolf, they began to be hungry again. The girl was very unhappy, and one day she sat there crying. Pretty soon, the boy said, "Sister, look at that antelope." "No," said the girl, "It is useless for me to look. Looking will do no good." --- "But look," said the boy, "perhaps it will fall down the way the wolf did." The girl finally looked, and the same thing happened to the antelope that happened to the wolf. They cut it up and made a bed for themselves out of the skin. They ate the flesh and fed the old dog the liver. The girl would chew up the pieces for the dog who had no teeth. Everytime they got hungry the same thing happened. They killed an elk this way, and a buffalo. They used the elk-hide for a shelter and added the buffalo hide to it later. They stayed there till winter came, and snow began to fall. They had only these two hides for shelter.

One night the girl went to bed and made a wish. She said, "I wish that I would see a lodge over there in the morning. I could sleep there with my brother and the dog and could have a bed in the back of the lodge. I could make my brother a bow and some arrows, so he could kill buffalo close to camp when they come to use the brush as a windbreak." She also wished that her brother would become a young man and that they would have meat racks in the camp.

In the morning, when the boy got up, he said, "Sister, there is our lodge over there now." It was just where the girl had wished. They moved their things over to it. They took the fire over, and when the boy went inside he had become a young man. That winter he killed many buffalo, and they had plenty of meat.

One night, as the girl was going to bed, she made another wish. She was talking to her brother when she made it. She said, "Brother, our father has treated us very badly. He made us eat our mother, and he had us tied up and deserted by the people. He has treated us badly, and I wish we had two bears that we could make eat our father.

The next morning, when the girl got up, she saw two bears sitting on either side of the lodge door. She said to them, "Hello my animals, rise and eat." Then she gave them food. She went out to one of the meat racks and pulled a piece of bloody fat from some meat that was hanging there. A raven was sitting in a tree near-by. She spoke to the raven, saying, "Come here. I want to send you on an errand." When the raven had come over to her, she said, "Go and look for the camp of my people. Fly about among the lodges calling and when the people come out and ask each other what you are doing and what you are carrying, drop this piece of fat where the crowd is gathered. Tell the people that you come from a place that has great scaffolds of meat." The raven took the piece of fat in his bill and flew away. He found the camp and flew about calling. A group of men that were sitting in the camp began to say, "What is that raven carrying?" The raven dropped the meat, and someone picked it up and said, "Why, this is fresh meat!" Then the raven said, "Those people that you threw away are still in camp and they have scaffolds of meat." Then the raven flew to the girl and told her what he had done.

An old man began to walk through the camp, crying out to the people and saying, "Those children that we threw away have plenty of meat. They are in the old camp. Now we must move back to it as quickly as we can." The people tore down their lodges and packed up and started back. Some of the young men went ahead in little groups of threes and fours and reached the children's camp before the others. When they arrived there the girl fed them and gave them meat to carry back to the main camp. All the trees about the lodge were covered with meat, and buffalo hides were stacked up in great piles. After a time, the whole village came to the place and camped close to the children's lodge. All the people began to come to the lodge to get food. The girl sent word to her father not to come until all the rest had come. When they had been supplied, he could come and take his time and not eat in a hurry. She said to the bears, "I am going to send you for your food last. After my father gets here and has eaten and goes out of the lodge, I will say, 'There is your food!'. When I say this, you eat him up."

In the evening when the last one of the people was leaving the lodge, she said to him, "Tell the people not to come here any more. My father is coming now." When the father came, they fed him, and he was glad. He said, "Oh, my children, you are living nicely here. You have plenty of meat and tongues and back fat." He didn't eat everything the girl had set in front of him. He said, "I will take this home for my breakfast." After he had gone out of the lodge to return to the camp, the girl said to the bears, "There is your food! Eat him up!" The bears sprang after the father and pulled him down. He called to his daughter to get the animals off, but she let them kill him there. The bears began to drag him back to the lodge. The girl said to them, "Take him off somewhere else and eat him, and what you don't eat throw into the stream." What the bears didn't eat, they threw into the stream. Then they washed their hands, and no one ever knew what had become of the father. Since that time bears have eaten human flesh when they get the chance.

The boy and the girl returned to the camp and lived there afterwards.

30. ROLLING ROCK

(Flathead)

Coyote and Fox went on from there to a place called Ross's Hole. Coyote had a fine new blanket. As they went along they saw a very nice big smooth round Rock. Coyote thought it was a very nice Rock. He said, "I think you are a very nice Rock. You're the nicest Rock I have ever seen. I guess I'll give you my blanket to keep you warm." So Coyote gave the blanket to Rock.

Then Coyote and Fox went on their way. Pretty soon it began to thunder and lightning. Coyote and Fox went under a tree for shelter. Now Coyote had no blanket to keep the rain off his nice beaded clothing, and he was afraid his clothes would get spoiled. He told Fox to go back and get the blanket from Rock. Fox went and asked Rock for the blanket, but Rock said, "No!" Then Fox came back and told Coyote. Coyote said, "Go back and ask Rock if I can't please have the blanket for a little while. I'll give it back to him after the rain is over." Fox went back and asked Rock again, but Rock said, "No, he can't have it. I want it myself." Then Fox went back and told Coyote what Rock had said. "Well," said Coyote, "he is awfully mean. I think he might let me have the blanket for just a little while. He never had a blanket before. Why should I work hard and get a blanket just to let him keep it? I won't do it. I'll take my blanket." So Coyote went back and jerked the blanket away from Rock.

Then all at once it cleared up. Coyote and Fox sat down to smoke. While they were smoking, they heard a crushing, crashing noise. They looked up and saw Rock come rolling toward them as hard as he could. They jumped and ran down the hill as fast as they could run. Rock was going awfully fast, and going downhill he got pretty close to them. Fox jumped into a hole in the side of the hill, and Rock just touched the tip of his tail as he went by. That is what made the tip of Fox's tail white.

Coyote went on down the hill, jumped into the river, and swam through and came up on the other side. He saw Rock go into the river and thought he would sink to the bottom, but Rock swam through all right, came up on the other side, and went after Coyote. Then Coyote ran for the thick timber. When he got to the middle of the thick woods, he lay down and went to sleep. Pretty soon he woke up and heard the trees crashing and crackling. Then he knew that Rock was still after him. Coyote jumped up and ran for the prairie. Rock came after him on the prairie. Coyote saw a big Bear, and Bear said to Coyote, "I'll save you." Pretty soon

Bear and Rock came together. Bear fell dead. Then Coyote saw a big Buffalo, and Buffalo said to Coyote, "I'll save you." Rock passed on. He struck Buffalo, and Buffalo fell dead.

Coyote ran on till he came to where two Old Women were standing. They had stone hatchets in their hands. They said to Coyote, "We'll save you." Coyote ran in between them, and Rock came right after him. Coyote heard the Old Women strike Rock with their hatchets. He turned and saw Rock lying on the ground, all broken to pieces.

Then Coyote noticed that he was in a big camp. Pretty soon he heard the Old Women say, "He looks nice and fat. We'll have something good for our supper now. Let's eat him right away." Coyote sat and studied. When Coyote wished for anything it always came to pass. So he wished that all the water would dry up. After he had made the wish, he said, "I am very thirsty. I wish you would let me get a good drink of water." --- The Old Women said, "There is plenty of water here. You may have a drink." But when they looked in the pails they found that every one was empty, and all the little streams close by were dry. Coyote said, "I know where there is a creek that has water in it. I will go and get some water for you." He took the pails and started off. When he got out of sight, he ran away. The Old Women waited for him for a long time. Then they began to blame each other for letting him get away. Pretty soon they got so angry, they killed each other.

Stories of a man who finds that his house is being put in order every day by an unknown visitor are not uncommon in North American mythology. The most famous is the Cree tale called Mudjikiwis, in which ten brothers find a girl taking care of their home. The eldest brother eventually becomes jealous of the brother that marries the girl, attempts to win the girl, shoots her, and frightens her away. There then ensues a pursuit of the girl that is remarkably close to the European Swan Maiden story. Tale 31, The Man Who Married a Branch, is far less pretentious than Mudjikiwis, ends quickly and happily, and is in no way suspect of foreign influences. However, the tale is not widely known either.

31. THE MAN WHO MARRIED A BRANCH

(Lillooet)

Once a man lived alone in an underground house. All the other people in the land lived very far away. He longed to have a wife, but did not know where to get one. At last he made up his mind to make a tree-branch his wife. He travelled around for many days, breaking branches from trees. He wanted one that would have a hole in it when he broke it off from the tree. At last he found one that suited him. He carried it home and treated it as though it were his wife. He talked to it, and then changing his voice talked again as if it were answering him. He had intercourse with it, and when he went out he covered it over with a blanket and left food and water beside it.

A woman who lived in a distant country knew how the man was acting and went to see him. She reached the house when he was away, put it in order, drank the water, and ate the food that had been left for the branch wife. As evening came on, she lighted the fire. When the man came home, she hid herself and watched. The man went hunting for four consecutive days and always found the house arranged, the food and water gone when he came back. He thought to himself, "My branch-wife must be doing this. She must be getting alive." And he was glad that his wife was becoming useful and could eat and drink.

The next night, before the hunter came home, the woman threw the branch in the fire. When he arrived and could not find the branch, he wept and lamented, saying, "My loss is great. My wife must have fallen into the fire while she was climbing the ladder to go and get water. What shall I do for a wife?" Then the woman laughed at him from where she was hidden. She stepped towards him and asked him who he was crying for. She said to him, "I burned the branch, and now I will be your wife." She told him the whole story, and he was glad to have a real woman. They lived together and had many children.

The Eskimo are generally set apart from all other American aborigines and have a separate mythology. In it the only story that resembles an origin myth is the story of _Sedna_, mistress of the underworld, in which the beginnings of fish and sea-animals are accounted for. The other tales are similar to _The Origin of the Narwhal_, which is printed here, and feature accounts concerning the origin of man, natural elements, the sun and the moon. These stories do not fall together in a coherent pattern, however. Many of the stories, like Tale 32, seem disjointed and are a mixture of violence, resuscitations, and journeys to strange lands.

32. THE ORIGIN OF THE NARWHAL

(Eskimo)

There was a blind boy who lived with his mother and sister. They went to a place where there was no one and lived alone. One day, when they were in their tent, a bear came up to it. Though the boy was blind he had a bow, and the woman aimed it at the bear for him. The arrow struck the bear and killed it. The mother, however, deceived her son and told him he had missed it. She cut it up and then cooked it. The young man now smelled the bear-meat and asked his mother whether it was not bear he was smelling. She, however, told him he was wrong. Then she and her daughter ate it, but she would give him nothing. His sister put half her food in her dress secretly to give him later. When her mother asked her why she was eating so much, the girl answered she was hungry. Later, when the mother was away, she gave the meat to her brother. In this way he discovered that his mother had deceived him. Then he wished for another chance to kill something, when he might not be deceived by his mother.

One day, when he was out of doors, a large loon came down to him and told him to sit on its head. The loon then flew with him toward its nest, and finally brought him to it, on a large cliff. After they had reached the cliff, it began to fly again, and took him to a pond. The loon then dived with him, in order to make him recover his eyesight. It would dive and ask him whether he was smothering. When he answered that he was, it took him above the surface to regain his breath. Thus they dived, until the blind boy could see again. His eyesight was now very strong. He could see as far as the loon, and could even see where his mother was, and what she was doing. Then he returned. When he came back his mother was afraid, and tried to excuse herself, and treated him with much consideration.

One day he went narwhal hunting, using his mother to hold the line. "Spear a small narwhal," his mother said, for she was afraid a large one would drag her into the water. He speared a small one, and she pulled it ashore. Then they ate its blubber. The next time two appeared together, a small white whale and a large narwhal. "Spear the small one again," she told him. But he speared the large one, and when it began to pull he let go the line, so that his mother was dragged along, and forced to run, and pulled into the water. "My knife," she cried. She kept calling for her knife, but he did not throw it to her, and she was drawn

131

away and drowned. She turned into a narwhal; her hair, which she wore twisted to a point, became a tusk.

After this, the man who had recovered his sight and the sister went away. Finally they came to a house. The brother was thirsty and wanted water. He asked his sister for some, telling her to go to the house for it. She went up to it, but was at first afraid to go in. "Come in, come in!" cried the people inside, who were murderous adlit. When she entered, they seized her and ate her. She had stayed away a long time, and finally her brother went to look for her. He entered the house, but could not find her. An old man there, after having eaten of her, tried to say he did not have her and did not know where she was. The brother, however, kept stabbing the inmates of the house with a tusk he had, trying to make them confess, but in vain, finally killing them all. Then the brother put her bones together and went away carrying them on his back. Then the flesh grew on the bones again, and soon she spoke, "Let me get up!" But he said to her, "Don't get up!" At last she got up, however. Then they saw a great many people and soon reached them. By this time his sister had recovered. She ate and went into a house. She married there and soon had a child. Her brother also married.

The rest of the tales in this anthology involve tricks and pranks played by particular tricksters in their wanderings about the world or by one animal or another. Many of the incidents ascribed here to a certain character are as often ascribed to some other figure. Many of the events and situations are known to many tribes over a wide area. Although trickster tales were discussed in the Introduction, it would be well to remind the reader here that these pranks are usually played by figures of great stature in the tribal mythology and frequently illustrate the wrong way of going about things.

Tale 33, Grizzly Bear and Doe, was widespread in California in this form. Tale 34, Turtle's War Party, was known to most of the Plains tribes. It contains a "mock plea" ending that will remind the reader of The Tar-Baby. In it, the traditional emnity of the Thunderers and the Water Monsters is stressed. This accounts for the manner in which the Indians persuade Turtle to let Otter go. Tale 35, Porcupine and Caribou, was most frequently told among the Plains and Plateau tribes concerning Coyote, Porcupine, and Buffalo. The Carrier have simply substituted animals more common to their area.

The first portion of Tale 36, Coyote Borrows Feathers, contains a world-wide motif, of which this version is typically American Indian. The text as printed in JAF continues on through some rather pointless adventures that Coyote has in pursuit of Duck and the girl. As this portion of the story is not regularly a part of the borrowed feathers incident, it has been omitted here.

Tale 37, Why the Buzzard is Bald, in one of the liveliest explanation stories in the world. It was common to most the woodland tribes. Tale 38, The Hoodwinked Dancers, Tale 39, The Bungling Host, and Tale 40, The Eye-Juggler, were known over most of the Continent. The tricks played in the bungling host story varied widely from group to group, however, and the version here is a composite of two texts collected by Lowie at separate times. White-man, in The Eye-Juggler, is an Indian mythological figure and not an American, of course.

The adventures of Naniboju, Nanabozho, or Nanibush and Whiskey Jack or Wisakedjak are pretty much interchangeable. Naniboju was a powerful Culture Hero and Trickster of the Algonguin-speaking Indians. A great transformer, he was frequently associated with the hare and the wolverine. Whiskey Jack was an identical Cree and Saulteaux Ojibwa hero. The events presented in Tales 41 and 42, as well as those attributed to Coyote in Tale 43, are extremely well-known. The two attributed to Whiskey Jack were actually taken from two different tribes, the Plains Ojibwa and the Plains Cree, at separate times. However, so universal are the events they can be combined here without distortion. Note that the incidents of Tales 41, 42, and 43 come from the Lake Ontario region, from the Western Canadian Plains, and from California, which is an indication of how widespread such material was.

The Iowa Ishijinki, was quite like Naniboju and Whiskey Jack. Although the incidents given in Tales 44 and 45 were not as popular as those in Tales 41-43, they were common enough.

33. GRIZZLY BEAR AND DOE

(Lassik)

Grizzly Bear and Doe, the two wives of Chickenhawk, were pounding acorns. When they had finished one of them said, "Let's go down to the creek and leach the meal." While they were waiting for the meal to soak, they agreed to lice one another's heads. Doe looked first at Grizzly's hair. "You have no lice," she said. "Well, then," said Grizzly, "I will look in yours." When she reached Doe's neck in her search she sprinkled in some sand. "You have many lice;" she said, "I will chew them." "Ukka! Ukka!" cried Doe, "hold on there." But Grizzly bit off her head, killing her. Taking Doe's head and lots of acorn meal, she went back to the house. She put the head in the fire and when the eyes burst with the heat she told the children it was only the white oak log cracking in the fire. "I think it is our mother's head," said one of Doe's children. "Go a long way off and play," said Grizzly. They heard their mother's hair say, "You won't be permitted to live long."

The two bear children and the two fawns went out to play. "Let's play smoke each other out in this hollow log," suggested the fawns. The bears agreed, and the fawns went in first. "That's enough; that's enough," they cried. Then they told the bears, "Now you go in." The fawns fanned the smoke into the log until the bears were smothered. Going back to the house, one of them held out her hand and said, "Here is a skunk we killed in a log." "Very well," said Grizzly. Then the other fawn held out her hand and said, "Here is a skunk we killed in a log." "Thank you, my niece. After a while I will make a meal upon them," replied Grizzly. She took the young bears and began to eat them.

"She is eating her children," she heard someone say. "What did you say?" she asked. "First you killed a person, and now you are eating your own children." She ran after the fawns who had been taunting her. When she came near them she called in a pleasant voice, "Well, come home." They ran up on a ridge and barely escaped being caught. Finally they came to a place where Crane was fishing in the river. "Grandfather, put your neck across and let us go over on it. An old woman is after us. Put your neck across."

They crossed over safely and running to the top of a ridge hid in a hole in a rock. When Grizzly came, she also asked Crane to put his neck across. Crane put his neck out again, but when she was halfway over he gave it a sudden twist. Grizzly fell off. She went floating down the middle of the stream.

135

34. TURTLE'S WAR-PARTY

(Plains Ojibwa)

Once Snapping Turtle thought he would go to war. So he turned to the north and began to sing, "Who will go with me to hunt the enemy?" Presently Owl came up. "I will go!" he cried. "What will you do if we meet the enemy?" asked Turtle. Owl hovered noiselessly about for a moment and then pounced down to earth. "Oh, you are no good! You would be shot at once!" cried Turtle, sending him off.

Then Turtle faced to the east and began to sing, "Who will go with me to face the enemy?" In a short time Raven appeared. "I will go!" he cried. "What can you do if we meet the enemy?" asked Turtle. Raven circled and swooped down out of the sky. "Oh, you won't do!" said Turtle. "You would be shot in an instant."

So he turned to the South and began to sing, "Who will go with me to face the enemy?" Instantly Hawk came dashing up. "I will go!" he cried. "What would you be able to do if we should meet the enemy?" asked Turtle. The hawk flew high into the heavens and pounced down with great speed. "Oh, you are no good!" said Turtle. "You are too slow; you would be shot at once."

So Turtle faced to the west and sang, "Who will go with me to face the enemy?" By and by Small Tortoise came crawling up. "I will go!" he said. "What would you be able to do if we should meet the enemy?" asked Turtle. Straightway Small Tortoise thrust his neck in and out of his shell, snapping and drawing back. "Oh yes, that's fine! If you are hit with a tamahawk you will never be hurt!" cried Turtle in delight. So he called to him a whole army of small tortoises and led them away.

At night the warriors arrived at the camp of the enemy. They hid in the brush and held council until early dawn, when they rushed to the attack. Fortunately for the enemy, an old woman had arisen very early and gone out to ease herself. As she was arranging her clothes, she heard a scuffling and scratching in the leaves, and looking up, she saw the army bearing down on her. Hastily fixing her dress, she snatched up one of the foremost tortoises and ran home shouting, "Get your bags, get your bags! The turtles are upon us!"

All the people sprang from their beds, snatched up their bags, ran out, and captured the whole army. While they were busy catching the warriors, Snapping Turtle ran back around the other way into the village and entered one of the tents. There he saw a large

wooden bowl turned upside down. He crawled under it. Meantime the enemy carried the other turtles home and began to cook
and eat them. A little boy was sent to get the wooden bowl. When
he lifted it up, there was Snapping Turtle. No one could guess
where he came from.

When Turtle was captured, all the elders were called to
counsel how to kill him. "Oh, throw him in the fire!" said one.
"Better not," replied Turtle, "I'll throw brands out at you." ---
"Oh, perhaps that is so!" said the counsellors. "Let's boil him!"
--- "Better not," said Turtle, "I'll splatter hot water all over you."
--- "Let's take an axe and chop him up! suggested another. ---
"Oh, you can't do that!" said Turtle. "Your women will have no
axes to use. They will break them on my back." Just then a little
boy who was standing in the door said, "Oh, I know what to do with
him! Throw him in the river." Then Turtle began to feign terror
and wail, "Oh, don't do that, that's what I am afraid of." --- "Oh,
then that's what we shall do with you!" cried the enemy. So they
grabbed him by the tail and legs and dragged him, kicking and
struggling, down to the river, where they threw him in. This was
what he wanted.

There were two young girls undergoing their puberty-fast together in a little lodge out in the woods. That night Snapping
Turtle crawled out of the water and went there. He peeped into
the lodge, and he saw the girls lying, one on each side, sound
asleep. He drew his knife and crawled in. He cut off the head
of the first girl, and then the other. Then he scalped them and
went back to the river.

Early in the morning Turtle crawled on a big rock that stood
in the water. Soon the people heard him singing his war-song, "My
legs are half crooked." The mother of the two girls he had killed
took her comb and went out to dress their hair. When she arrived
at the lodge she found them murdered, with their heads lying one
on each side of the door. She dropped the door-covering and rushed
home to tell her husband. "And the one who did it is singing over
there!"

Then the enemy got together a big war-party and went down
to the river, where they could see Turtle sitting on the rock and
singing. It happened that Otter was married into the tribe at that
time. He volunteered to go and avenge the girls. So he led all
the people to the brink, took off all his clothes, and dived in and
swam. Snapping Turtle saw what was happening, so he jumped into
the water and swam to meet Otter. When Otter swam by over
him, he reached up and bit Otter's testicles. Otter screamed,

"Heuh-e! Snapping Turtle is biting me!" --- "Where?" shouted the people. "Breast!" yelled Otter. He should have shouted "Testicles", but he was ashamed because some of his wife's relatives were in the multitude. "Oh, where did you say?" --- "Oh, it's my testicles!" he cried at last. "He won't let me go till the Thunderers come."

The Indians tried to deceive Turtle. They got a tambourine drum and began to beat it in imitation of the Thunderers. As soon as Snapping Turtle heard them, he let go. Otter was badly hurt. When he got out of the water, he wrapped himself in a blanket and called his wife's sister to sew him up.

35. PORCUPINE AND CARIBOU

(Carrier)

Invitations had gone out for a potlatch and people from all parts began to travel towards the village where it was to be held. Two or three days after all the others had left, Porcupine started out alone. He travelled along the trail day after day until he reached a river which the people had crossed in canoes and on rafts. Porcupine had no axe to make a raft and was unable to cross. He waited on the bank until Caribou appeared. He said to Caribou, "My nephew, come and help me cross the river. Carry me over." Caribou agreed and said, "Stand on my back." Porcupine said, "I shall stand facing backwards." So Caribou started to swim across the river with Porcupine. But Porcupine twisted his tail around and drove it farther and farther into Caribou's belly. When they were approaching the other bank, Caribou said, "Something is sticking into me." But Porcupine answered, "It is only the babichi string of my belt that is tickling you." They had almost landed when Porcupine jabbed his tail right into Caribou's belly. Caribou shivered and threw Porcupine into the river. After being carried far down, he managed to land. Then he followed Caribou's tracks until he came upon the dead body. He sat down beside him, wondering what to do, as he had no knife to remove the hide. While he was thinking, a flock of ducks flew over him. Porcupine called out to them, "Ducks, lend me a knife." They threw him down a small flint knife, and he began to skin Caribou.

Wolverine came along and said, "My nephew, you are a good hunter. I see you have killed a big caribou." Porcupine said, "Yes, I have killed it." --- "I'll help you skin it," said Wolverine. "You don't know how to do it. You are cutting it wrong. Sit down and let me skin it for you." Porcupine sat down and Wolverine skinned the caribou. He cut off the legs, then took out the entrails and placed them before Porcupine, saying, "Wash these down at the river for me." Porcupine took them down to the river, ate nearly all the fat from them, and returned with the remainder. Wolverine said, "How come there is no fat left on them?" Porcupine answered, "A little fish in the river ate it." But the little fish heard him and called out, "Porcupine lies. He ate it himself." Wolverine then took his antler club and struck Porcupine on the head. Porcupine bristled, and the club striking his nose made the blood pour out. He fell down and pretended to be dead. Wolverine was glad, saying, "I am a good hunter. I killed a caribou and now I have killed a porcupine." He piled up all the caribou meat, covered it with the skin and packed on his back just enough meat for a load. Then he placed Porcupine on the top of his pack and started out. As he walked Porcupine caught at the brush, and when Wolverine tried to break free let go suddenly and made Wolverine fall. He himself was flung far in front. After this had happened several times, Wolverine became angry and said, "I'll bring my wife and children here." He cached his pack and Porcupine and started for his home. As soon as he had gone, Porcupine jumped up, took the pack, and returned to where the rest of the caribou lay.

Near the caribou were some large trees. Porcupine carried all the meat up one of them, stripped the bark from the trunk so that Wolverine could not climb up, and rubbed caribou grease on it. Then he went to the top of the tree and ate. Soon Wolverine returned with his wife and children and was surprised to find the meat gone. One of his children said, "Father, there is someone up that tree." Wolverine looked up and seeing Porcupine tried to climb the tree. But it was too slippery, and he fell again and again. Porcupine called down, "Camp alongside the tree and I will drop some meat down for you." Wolverine and his family camped under the tree, and Porcupine dropped down some meat for them to eat. There they stayed for a long time. Then Porcupine said, "Sleep together and cover yourselves with a blanket. I'll throw you down some large pieces of meat." But instead he sharpened all the ribs and the backbone of Caribou and hurled them down. Wolverine was peeping through a tiny hole in the blanket and leaped aside, but his wife and children were killed.

Wolverine wept and said, "My nephew, I am in trouble now and hungry. Help me. My wife and children are dead." Porcupine descended the tree, took Wolverine on his back and packed him up the tree. There he cooked some meat and gave it to Wolverine. Wolverine tried to seize Porcupine, but Porcupine leaped from tree to tree. Wolverine tried to follow him, but the distance was so great that he fell to the ground and was killed. Porcupine then ate him and all of his family. He then made a club of the caribou antler and went on towards the village where the potlatch was being held. As he approached a large village, someone saw him and said, "Here comes Porcupine." He entered a house full of gamblers and was offered a seat. But he sat by the door and presently asked, "Let someone tell me my name." One man said, "I know. Your name is Porcupine." Porcupine hit him on the head with his club and killed him. Then he ran away to another village, where he sat down inside the door of another house filled with gamblers and asked the same question. This time the man said, "I know, it is Chief of the Foothills. Then Porcupine was satisfied and sat down in the place assigned to him.

36. COYOTE BORROWS FEATHERS

(Vintah Ute)

One day Coyote came to a big river. He wanted to be clean and not dirty anymore, so he jumped in and took a swim and washed himself. Then he ate some food and went to sleep in the brush and willows. He dreamt of birds --- eagles, hawks, geese, and ducks --- and when he awoke he saw a number of geese on the lake. He went down to the shore and asked the geese how they flew, how their feathers moved, and how they flew so easily without falling down. "Yes," said the geese, "It's just as easy as walking." Then Coyote said, "Give me some feathers so I can fly too." --- "No," said the geese, "maybe you will fall in, and maybe you will make a noise all the time. You will go off somewhere and get lost. Geese keep together all the time and never stray." --- "But I will go with you," said Coyote, "then the Indians will say, 'How nice that looks!' I will go ahead. I know the way best."

Then the geese said, "All right," and each goose gave him some feathers. They stuck the feathers over him until he was completely covered, and then they said, "Now try them!" Coyote tried and flew easily over the lake without falling in. He flew easily and lightly. "That's all right," said the geese. "Now we will go." They all started up, crying as they went. The geese cried only as they rose and descended, but Coyote cried all the time. He imitated the cry of the geese, "Ai, ai ai!" They flew high in the air and then came down on the banks of a big river. When they had all alighted, the geese said, "Why do you cry all the time?" Coyote replied, "I am practicing Otherwise I might forget it. So I keep trying." But the geese answered, "Well, we want no more crying. Now we are going again, and if you keep on crying, we will pull all your feathers out." --- "All right," said Coyote, so they started again. They all cried as they rose, but Coyote kept on crying. Then they gathered around him and pulled all his feathers out. He fell down a long way to the ground and was badly hurt. However, he got up and said, "Well my friend, I'll go along the ground. I like it better."

The geese said, "We are going to see the Utes." Then they left Coyote behind. When they arrived the Utes were engaged in a great fight with the Sioux. Coyote lay down and slept for a little while, when he came up the fight was over. The geese had stayed to the end, and when Coyote arrived they gave him a girl they had rescued. Coyote said, "What's the reason they stopped so soon? Why don't they come back?" But he took the girl and went to his home with her. Soon a snowstorm began, and she made him a brush house. Coyote carelessly left a pointed stick upright in the ground. The girl came in and sat on it. It went up inside her. She began to cry, and Coyote said, "Something has hurt my girl. I will hunt for a doctor." Before long he found Duck Doctor and said to him, "My girl is hurt, and I am looking for a doctor." Duck Doctor said, "Go look for another doctor also." So Coyote went. Meanwhile Duck went to Coyote's home and said to the girl, "Where are you sick?" The girl replied, "A stick has gone inside of me." Then Duck pulled the stick out and poked it into the bottom of the fire.

Soon Coyote returned home. Duck did not tell him what the trouble was, but said, "You better go and get water. Get it from the bottom of the lake, in the middle." But Coyote thought, "Why does he want me to get it way out there? There's too much water there. I'll get it closer to shore." So he got a jar and waded into the water up to his knees. Then he reached out and filled the jar with water and took it to Duck. Duck asked, "Where did you get this water?" --- "Oh, said Coyote, "I stood so deep in the water. I got it right there." --- "I told you in the middle," said Duck and threw the water away. "All right," said Coyote, and he went off again. This time he waded in up to his hips and got water. But when he brought it back, Duck looked at it and said, "This water was too near the shore. I told you way out in the middle, in deep water." So Coyote went again. He walked till the water reached his breast and brought water from there. But Duck only said, "No, that is not deep enough water. I told you way down in the middle." Coyote answered, "All right, I'll do it," and

he went again. He went in up to his nose and got a jar of water.
But Duck just looked at it and said to him, "No, go far down in
deep water. This water is too close to shore. It is not good."
--- "All right," said Coyote, "I'll do it." This time he walked
until the water covered his head, and then he kept on much farther.
He filled his jar with water and waded out again. But he slipped
on the mud on his way out and spilled all the water. Then he
went in again, a long distance after the water had covered his head.
He got a fresh jar of water and carried it safely home. He entered
the house and said, "I got your water way down deep in the middle."
Then he looked around. Duck and the girl were gone.

Then Coyote knew that Duck had stolen his girl in this way.
"What's the reason," he thought, "that he stole my girl." He sat
down and thought about it. "Which way did he go?" he thought.
Then far down in the fire he heard a noise. "Psst!" It was the
stick. He thought, "What's the cause of that noise in there?" Then
he poked the fire and pulled the stick out. "What kind of stuff is
that?" he thought. "Maybe it is good to eat." So he cooled it in
water. "That's my dinner," said Coyote. Then he began to eat it.
At the first bite he cried, "Wu, wu, wu!" But he kept on till he
had finished it. Then he knew what all the trouble was about and
why his girl had been sick.

37. WHY THE BUZZARD IS BALD

(Iowa)

As Ishjinki was travelling he came to a place where he saw
Buzzard flying above him. "Oh, grandfather," he said, "how much
fun you must have up there in the air. There is nothing that can
hurt you, and you can see everywhere. I wish I could get up as
high as that and see as far as you do." --- "You would never get
used to it, my grandson," said Buzzard. "You belong down there
and I belong up here. I'd rather you stayed where you are."

But Ishjinki begged and teased Buzzard, until finally the bird
took him up a little ways and returned. Then Ishjinki asked Buzzard
to take him higher. This happened four times. The last time
Buzzard took Ishjinki very high, so that Ishjinki cried "Wahaha"
every time that Buzzard dipped and soared. Finally Buzzard went
down close over the tops of the timber until he saw a hollow stump.
He tipped his wings, and threw Ishjinki headfirst into the stump.
Ishjinki was stuck there.

It just happened there was a hunting party of Sauk camping near-by, and some of their women came very close to the tree as they were gathering firewood. Ishjinki was able to see them through a crack. He called out to them, "Big male raccoon in here!" "Listen!" said one of the women, and again Ishjinki called, "Big male raccoon in here!" This time the women heard him plainly. They went up to the tree, and Ishjinki put his coonskin up to a crack so that they could see it plainly. They cut a hole in the stump so they could see better. "There it is! It's big!" called Ishjinki to encourage them. They chopped the hole still larger. At last, it was big enough, and Ishjinki said, "Oh my granddaughters, it's me. Let me out." --- "Oh, it's our grandfather," said the women, and Ishjinki jumped out. "Haa, I feel good now," he said. "Now you must dance, and I'll sing for you." They got their axes and held them, while Ishjinki sang, "Big male raccoon in here! big male raccoon in here!"

Ishjinki was very angry at Buzzard, so he made a trap to catch him. He pretended he was a dead horse and lay still until the crows picked at his rump. Buzzard appeared, but even though Ishjinki tried his trick three times he could not fool him. The fourth time he tried being a dead elk. The birds came and ate most of his rump. The crows even went in and out of his body. At last Buzzard came and pecked at Ishjinki's rump. Finally, he stretched his head and reached way inside. All at once Ishjinki closed the opening. "Now I've got you," he exclaimed, and he walked off with Buzzard dangling from his rear. He kept Buzzard there for a long time. Finally he said, "I'll let you go now. You have paid for your trick." Buzzard then pulled his head out, but he has been bald and smelly ever since.

38. THE HOODWINKED DANCERS

(Comanche)

Coyote met Skunk. "Halloo, brother! I am very hungry. Let's work some scheme to get something to eat! I will lead the way; do you follow?" --- "Well, I will do whatever you propose." --- "Over there is a prairie dogs' village. We will stay here until daylight. In the morning you will go to the prairie dog village and play dead. I will come later and say to the prairie dogs, 'Come let us have a dance over the body of our dead enemy!' Well, go there, puff yourself up and play dead." Skunk followed the directions. Coyote got to the prairie dogs. "Come, we will have a dance. Stop up your holes tight, let everyone come here. Our enemy lies dead before us. Do you all stand in a big circle and dance with closed eyes? If anyone looks, he will turn into something bad." As they were dancing, Coyote killed one of them. "Well, now all open your eyes! Look at this one. He opened his eyes and died. Now, all of you close your eyes and dance again. Don't look, or you will die." They began to dance once more, and Coyote began killing them. At last one of them looked. "Oh, he is killing us!" Then all the survivors ran for their holes. Coyote and Skunk gathered all the corpses and piled them up by a creek. They built a fire and cooked them.

    "Well," said Coyote, "let's run a race for them! The one that wins shall have all the good fat ones." --- "Oh," replied Skunk, "you are too swift. I am a slow runner and can never beat you." --- "Well, I will tie a rock to my foot." --- "If you tie a big one, I will race with you." They were to run around a hill. Coyote said, "Well, go on ahead; I will catch up to you." Skunk began to run. Coyote tied a rock to his foot and followed. Coyote said, "The one that is behind shall make a big fire, so there will be lots of smoke and we will be able to see where he is." Skunk got far ahead and turned aside to hide. When Coyote had run past him, Skunk turned back to the meat-pile. Looking back, he saw a big column of smoke rising on the other side of the hill. He took all the meat and carried it home. He cut off all the tails and left them sticking out, with two poor little prairie dogs for Coyote. Coyote thought Skunk was ahead of him. As he ran along, he said to himself, "I wonder where that fool is? I did not know that he could outrun me." He got back to the pile and saw the tails sticking out. He seized one, and it slipped out. He tried another one. "Oh, they are well cooked!" He tried another one. Then he got suspicious. He took a stick and raked up the fireplace, but could only find two lean prairie dogs. He thought someone must have stolen the meat. He ate the two lean prairie dogs. Skunk, lying in his den, was watching him. As Coyote was standing to look around, Skunk threw one of the prairie dog bones at him. Coyote then spied him lying in his camp. He saw all the meat around him. "Give me some of them!" --- "No, we have run a race for them. I beat you. I am going to eat them all." Coyote begged him in vain for some food. Skunk ate it all. He was a better trickster than Coyote.

39. THE BUNGLING HOST

(Southern Ute)

Beaver wanted to live near a creek. He put a dam there and swam about inside. He had four children. One day Wolf came along and entered his house. Beaver called two of his sons, killed both, and cooked them for dinner. He took the food to Wolf, asking him to pile up the bones and not to throw them outside. Wolf ate up everything and piled up the bones, which Beaver put into a pan and threw into the creek, whereupon the boys were restored to life and swam around again.

Then Wolf invited Beaver to visit him on the following day. Wolf moved to a little stream and put up a house near-by. He also had four boys. Beaver came in and sat down. Wolf called out two of his boys, killed, skinned, and boiled them. Then he took the dish and put it in front of Beaver, who said, "No thanks, I ate a lot just before leaving." --- "I think you are following in my tracks," said Wolf. --- "Do you and your wife eat this food yourselves," said Beaver. Wolf took it and threw it in the water, but the bones just sank and his children did not survive. Then he asked Beaver how to resusitate them. Beaver said, "I wish the boys were alive again." Then they were alive again.

The next time Wolf visited Mountain Goat, who was making arrows. He sat down. Mountain Goat took a bow and two arrows, stepped outdoors, and discharged one arrow so that it struck his buttocks and stuck in the kidneys. He took it out and both kidneys were on it. He shot off his second arrow and got flesh from about his lungs. "Cook it for Wolf." Wolf ate it all up and invited his host for the next day. He made arrows like Mountain Goat's and shot them into the air, but was scared and dodged both of them. "How do you do it?" --- "Oh, just the same way." He tried again and shot his sides. He took out his own flesh, but when he offered it to his guest, Mountain Goat said, ,"No thanks, I ate just before leaving." Wolf ate the meat with his wife.

Next Wolf visited Wild Goose. He got to a valley and met Wild Goose there. He sat down. Wild Goose rose, took a basket and a rock, went a short distance, sat down and put the basket under his left knee. He struck his left knee, making a sound, "aku'ru, ku'ru, ku'ru!" Wild turnips fell into the basket filling it. He brought them back, poured water on them, boiled them, and served the dish to Wolf who ate and liked it. When Wild Goose came, Wolf tried to strike himself in the same way, but was afraid to do it. Then Wild Goose wished he would hit himself and get a very small turnip. This is what happened. It was cooked for the guest, but Wild Goose said, "No, I never eat at a strange house; I had lunch just before leaving." Wolf said, "That's just the same way I do myself."

40. EYE-JUGGLER

(Cheyenne)

There was a man who could send his eyes out of his head onto the limb of a tree and call them back again by saying "eyes hang upon a branch." White-man saw him doing this and came to him crying. He wanted to learn this too. The man taught him, but warned him not to do it more than four times in one day. White-man went off along the river. When he came to the highest tree he could see, he sent his eyes to the top. Then he called them back. He thought he could do this as often as he wished, disregarding the warning. The fifth time his eyes remained fastened to the limb. All day he called, but the eyes began to swell and spoil, and flies gathered on them. White-man grew tired and lay down, facing his eyes, still calling for them. But they never came, and he cried.

At night he was half asleep, when a mouse ran over him. He closed his lids so that the mice would not see that he was blind, and lay still in order to catch one. At last, one sat on his breast. He kept quiet to let it become used to him, and the mouse went onto his face and tried to cut his hair for its nest. Then it licked his tears, and let its tail hang in his mouth. He closed his mouth and caught the mouse. He seized it tightly, and made it guide him about, telling it of his misfortune. The mouse said it could see the eyes and that they had swelled to an enormous size. It offered to climb the tree and get them for him. But White-man would not let it go. It tried to wiggle free, but he held it fast. Then the mouse asked on what condition he would release it, and White-man said, only if it gave him one of its eyes. So the mouse gave him one, and he could see again and let the mouse go. But the small eye was very far back in his socket, and he could not see very well with it.

A buffalo was grazing near-by, and as White-man stood near him crying, he looked on and wondered. White-man said, "Here is buffalo, who has the power to help me in my trouble." So the buffalo asked him what he wanted. White-man told him he had lost his eye and needed one. The buffalo took out one of his and put it in White-man's head. Now White-man could see far again. But the eye did not fit the socket. Most of it was outside. The eye from the mouse was far inside. Thus he remained.

41. ADVENTURES OF NANIBOJU

(Mississaga)

Naniboju was walking along a sandy shore, and after a while he became hungry. It was the fall of the year. He saw something moving towards him. It was a bear. He pulled up a sapling and, hiding himself, got ready to club the bear with it. When the bear came near enough he killed it with one blow. Then he built a fire, singed the bear's hair, and roasted the carcass. When it was sufficiently roasted, he cut the meat into small pieces with the intention of eating it leisurely. Just as he began to eat he was annoyed by the squeaking of a tree. To put a stop to it, he climbed the tree, and while trying to separate a split crotch, he got his hand caught. While he was trying to get his hand out, a pack of wolves ran down to the shore and came toward him. Naniboju kept working hard, trying to release his hand. Meanwhile the wolves began to eat his meal, paying no attention to him, although he shouted in order to scare them away. When the wolves had eaten up all the meat, he got his hand out of the crotch of the tree and came down. He found nothing left to eat, except the brain in the skull, which he couldn't get out. So he said, "I will change myself into a little snake and enter the skull and eat the brain." He did this, but when he got through eating he could not get out of the skull. So Naniboju went along the shore without seeing and soon fell into the lake. He swam under the water, and when he came up to the surface he heard voices saying, "There's a bear swimming in the lake; let's kill him!" There was a chase on the lake. When they got close they struck the bear on the head, splitting it open. Naniboju jumped out and got to dry land.

He continued his walk along the shore. The lake was calm, and the water began to freeze. Naniboju walked on the new ice and liked the sound the ice made. He saw Fisher coming towards him. Fisher made up his mind to make fun of Naniboju. Running to the shore, he peeled some basswood bark and with it tied two stones to his hind legs, so that every time he leaped the stones fell on the ice and made a musical sound. He ran towards Naniboju, who said, "Kwe! What are you doing with the basswood on your legs?"   "Nothing!" said Fisher.   "It's a nice day and I thought I would attach stones to my legs."   Fisher passed Naniboju, making music with the noise of stones falling on the new ice.   Naniboju listened to the ice-music for some time, until Fisher got out of sight on the lake.   Then he went to the shore, peeled basswood bark, tied two stones with it, and making two holes in his belly, put the bark through and tied it.   As he walked along, the stones made a loud noise on the ice, which pleased him at first.   But soon the stones made very little music, so he looked back.   He saw that the stones were far behind and that he was dragging part of his entrails on the ice.   He cut this part off and threw it on an elm-tree, saying, "My nephews will call that clinging vine.   They will use it when they have nothing else for food."

42. ADVENTURES OF WHISKEY JACK

(Plains Cree)

Once, when Whiskey Jack was walking along, he heard the noise of a great dance going on.   "Oh, I must go to that!" he thought.   So he hurried on until he saw a great crowd dancing.   He rushed to join them.   All day long they danced furiously, and all night long they stamped and bent without cease.   When dawn came, Whiskey Jack was worn out, and wished the dance were over.   When the sun rose, however, he discovered that he had not been dancing with people at all.   He found himself standing in the middle of a field of reeds, which he had seen blowing in the wind.   He slept for awhile, then he went on with his travels.

As he went along his rump began to annoy him by constantly breaking wind and scaring game that he was trying to sneak up on.   Enraged by this, he decided to punish his rump by sitting on a hot stone.   Thus he burned his rear severely.   Later on, when the wound began to heal, one of the scabs fell off in the snow.   Whiskey Jack was going back over the same ground, and he found it.   "Oh, my grandfather has been killing game, so my grandmother has plenty of smoked meat."   Picking up the scab, he began to eat it.   A bird near-by was convulsed with laughter.   "Oh, Whiskey Jack is eating a scab from his own rear!" he cried.   Whiskey Jack did not believe it.   "No, this is some of my grandmother's dried meat," he said.   But the bird told him the same thing over and over, till at last Whiskey Jack bit into a portion that convinced him.   In disgust, he threw the scab away and set off on his travels once more.

43. COYOTE'S AMOROUS ADVENTURES

(Shasta)

Once Coyote saw two girls walking along the road, and he said to himself, "I would like to have those girls. I wonder how I can get them!" A small creek ran parallel to the road. "I will go into the creek and turn into a salmon," said Coyote. He did so, and pretty soon the girls came to the creek. Upon seeing the salmon darting to and fro, one girl exclaimed, "Oh, here is a salmon! Let's catch it!" So the girls sat on opposite banks of the river, and the salmon swam back and forth, going in and out of their bodies. The elder girl said to her sister, "Do you feel anything queer?" Her sister answered, "Yes, I feel fine." Thereupon Coyote came out of the creek in his true form, and laughed at the girls, and said, "You thought it was a salmon, but I fooled you." The girls were angry and cursed him.

He kept on going downstream, and pretty soon he saw two girls digging camas on the other side of the river. He began to wonder how he could possess them. He stood on one bank and thrust himself across the river under water and entered the eldest girl. She tried to run away, but she could not move. The other thought that a bad spirit had caught her and stood back. She went and found an old witch, who was a sort of prophet, and told her about Coyote. The witch came and entered the water. She felt all over the girl's body until she finally located Coyote. "Oh, a bad spirit has you," she called, "get me my awl and corncrusher." The younger girl ran and brought the tools to the old woman. The witch then put the point of the awl against the part of Coyote that had entered the girl. She struck the awl with the crusher, so that Coyote was hurt and pulled himself back across the stream. The girl escaped, but Coyote just laughed.

44. TURTLE'S SACRED WAR BUNDLE

(Iowa)

Ishjinki went back to his friend Turtle, and they went around together a great deal, attending ball games and all manner of sports. One day Ishjinki said to Turtle, "My friend, I am the greatest man alive. I can fool anyone; I don't care who it is." To this Turtle replied, "You could never fool me." Ishjinki laughed, "Oh yes I could, if I really wanted to."

Wherever he went Turtle carried his sacred bundle with him; even at ball games he always had it. One evening Ishjinki decided to fool Turtle. Turtle was in a friend's lodge at the time. Ishjinki dressed as a girl and appeared as a beautiful Sauk woman, with trailing headdress and all. She sent someone into the lodge to say, "There is a beautiful Sauk girl here with no place to stay." The friend had brought her in, and as soon as Turtle laid eyes on her he desired her. He filled up his pipe to smoke, and when he drew on the mouthpiece he would chirp with his lips to attract her attention. At last the girl dropped her eyes. Turtle kept right on until she blushed and giggled. "Hehe, he always makes us laugh." Finally she left the lodge, and Turtle followed her and caught her. Ishjinki said, "I am a poor Sauk woman; I've no place to go. I am a wanderer, and I have no man either."

"Oh," said Turtle, "I have no woman. Let's sleep with each other." They talked for a while, and Turtle forgot his pipe. "You hold my sacred bundle," he said to Ishjinki, "and I will get my pipe and then we will go home." Turtle went for his pipe, and when he came back Ishjinki was gone with his sacred bundle. The Sauk girl had told Turtle her name. First Turtle began to call her by whispering "Sshh," very softly. Then he began to crawl around peering here and there under everything and whispering. Then he whistled her name. Then he began to call louder and louder, until at last he was frantic. While he was in this condition, Ishjinki came along in his proper dress.

"My friend," he said to Turtle, "what are you looking for a Sauk woman for? Here is your sacred bundle. Take it. I told you I could fool even you."

45. SLEEPING WITH A LOG

(Iowa)

While Ishjinki was going along he saw a woman coming. So he hid and disguised himself as a Sauk woman. He took balls from a sycamore tree and hung these all over his dress instead of jinglers. Then he went out and met the strange woman. "Oh, my sister-in-law," he said to her, which way are you travelling?" "Oh, I'm not sure," said the real woman; "I am looking for a place to die. My brothers never used to scold me, but lately they've been doing so. I'm angry so I am going off to die." "I am in the same fix. My brothers never used to scold me, but now they are abusing me, so I too am going off to die. Let's then travel together," said Ishjinki.

So they went along in each other's company. Towards evening they came to a good place to camp, so Ishjinki said, "Now sister-in-law, here is a good place to stay. Let us sleep here. We'll make a shelter, and one bed, so we can be together." They went in and lay down, and Ishjinki said, "Now let us tell stories." The woman said, "I don't know any, so you start, for I'd rather listen."

"Well," said Ishjinki, "once there was a village and in it dwelt a woman who had three or four brothers. These brothers abused her so that she wandered off to die, but on the way she met another woman who was in the very same plight, so they cast their lots together. When it came night, they made a camp and went to sleep, but it turned out that the second woman was really Ishjinki."

When Ishjinki finished the woman pretended that she was asleep, even when Ishjinki nudged her twice and spoke to her and told her that he was passionate. Ishjinki scuffled and wrestled with her nearly all night without success, and towards morning he was so tired he fell asleep. While he slept the woman got up and took an old rotten log that was full of ants and put it in his outstretched arms. Ishjinki began to fondle it, and pretty soon the ants began to bite him. "Oh, quit now, let me sleep," he said, thinking it was the woman. But the woman had fled. At last the ants bit him so hard that he awoke and was very angry. "Oh waaaa!" he exclaimed.

The chart below will give the reader pertinent bibliographical material and facts concerning the tales included in this book. Tribal ranges are in terms of modern geography. Linguistic stock is a convenient means of broad classification for the myriads of American Indian tribes.

Tale	Published in *JAF*	Original Editor	Tribe	Linguistic Stock	Tribal Range
1. The Emergence	1929,3-6, 11-13	Elsie C. Parsons from the collection of Alexander Stephen	Hopi	Shoshonean	No. Arizona
2. The Earthdiver	1923,305	Edward W. Gifford	Western Mono	Shoshonean	California
3. Ouiot and Frog	1906,59	Constance G. DuBois	San Luiseño	Shoshonean	So.California
4. Theft of Fire	1924,117	Robert Lowie	Southern Paiute	Shoshonean	Southwestern Utah
5. Theft of Light	1919,204	James A. Teit	Tahltan	Athapascan	South Alaska and British Columbia
6. How the Four Winds Were Created	1928,106	Paul Radin and A.B. Reagan	Ojibwa or Chippewa	Algonquin	Western Great Lakes
7. Coyote Arranges the Seasons of the Year	1915,228	Leo J. Frachtenberg	Shasta	Hokan	No. California
8. Origin of the Pleiades	1900,281	W. M. Beauchamp	Onondaga	Iroquoian	New York and S.E. Canada
9. The Girl Who Married a Dog	1900,181	A. L. Kroeber	Cheyenne	Algonquin	Wyoming and South Dakota
10. The Deer and the Rainbow	1899,123	William E. Connelley	Wyandot or Huron	Iroquoian	Quebec
11. The Frogs in the Moon	1902,298	James A. Teit	Lillooet	Salish	British Columbia
12. Afterbirth and Lodge Boy	1904,153	George A. Dorsey	Wichita	Caddoan	Oklahoma and Kansas
13. Loon Woman	1915,212	Leo J. Frachtenberg	Shasta	Hokan	No. California
14. Coyote Kills the Sucking Monster	1901,240	Louisa McDermott	Flathead	Salish	Western Montana
15. Walking Skeleton	1923,313	Edward W. Gifford	Western Mono	Shoshonean	California
16. Bloodclot	1924,44	Robert Lowie	Ute	Shoshonean	Utah
17. The Story of Sweet Medicine	1908,271	George B. Grinnell	Cheyenne	Algonquin	Wyoming and So.Dakota
18. Yellowtop-to-Head Woman	1907,173	George B. Grinnell	Cheyenne	Algonquin	Wyoming and So. Dakota
19. The Origin of Corn	1890,214	Mrs. W.Wallace Brown	Wabanaki or Abenaki	Algonquin	No. New England
20. Forgetting the Song	1918,223	Elsie C. Parsons	Zuñi	Zuñian	New Mexico
21. The Conquering Gambler	1921,233	James A. Teit	Tahltan	Athapascan	So. Alaska and British Columbia
22. Star Husband	1897,39	Franz Boas	Sekani	Athapascan	British Columbia
23. Northern Lights	1890,213	Mrs. W. Wallace Brown	Wabanaki or Abenaki	Algonquin	No. New England
24. The Land of the Dead	1909,37	Leo J. Frachtenberg from the collection of Harry H. St. Clair, II	Coos	Kusan	Oregon
25. Water Jar Boy	1943,69	Reprinted in *JAF* by Gladys Reichard from the collection of Elsie C. Parsons	Tewa, living among the Hopi	Tanoan	No. Arizona
26. The Sun-Snare	1928,272	D. S. Davidson	Tête de Boule	Algonquin	Quebec
27. The Lecherous Father and His Daughter	1924,28	Robert Lowie	Southern Ute	Shoshonean	So. Utah
28. The Toothed Vagina	1928,256	Jean Sapir	Yurok	Algonquin, Ritwan, or Independent	No. California
29. Rolling Skull	1903,108	George B. Grinnell	Cheyenne	Algonquin	Wyoming and So. Dakota
30. Rolling Rock	1901,245	Louisa McDermott	Flathead	Salish	Western Montana

Tale	Published in *JAF*	Original Editor	Tribe	Linguistic Stock	Tribal Range
31. The Man Who Married a Branch	1912,309	James A. Teit	Lillooet	Salish	British Columbia
32. The Origin of the Narwhal	1899,169	A. L. Kroeber	Eskimo	Eskimoan	No.Canada and Alaska
33. Grizzly Bear and Doe	1906,135	Pliny E. Goddard	Lassik	Athapascan	California
34. Turtle's War Party	1919,297	Alanson Skinner	Plains Ojibwa	Algonquin	Saskatchewan and Manitoba
35. Porcupine and Caribou	1934,250	Diamond Jenness	Carrier	Athapascan	British Columbia and Alberta
36. Coyote Borrows Feathers	1910,312	J. Alden Mason	Ute	Shoshonean	Utah
37. Why Buzzard is Bald	1925,486	Alanson Skinner	Iowa	Siouan	Iowa
38. The Hoodwinked Dancers	1909,273	Robert Lowie from the collection of Harry H. St. Clair,II	Comanche	Shoshonean	Texas
39. The Bungling Host	1924,21, 23	Robert Lowie	Ute	Shoshonean	Utah
40. The Eye-Juggler	1900,168	A. L. Kroeber	Cheyenne	Algonquin	Wyoming and So. Dakota
41. Adventures of Naniboju	1892,292	Alexander F. Chamberlain	Mississaga	Algonquin	North of Lake Ontario
42. Adventures of Whiskey Jack	1916,351; 1919,289	Alanson Skinner	Plains Cree and Plains Ojibwa	Algonquin	Saskatchewan and Manitoba
43. Coyote's Amorous Adventures	1915,222	Leo J. Frachtenberg	Shasta	Hokan	No.California
44. Turtle's Sacred War-Bundle	1925,490	Alanson Skinner	Iowa	Siouan	Iowa
45. Sleeping With a Log	1925,488	Alanson Skinner	Iowa	Siouan	Iowa

OTHER COLLECTIONS OF INDIAN TALES PUBLISHED BY THE AMERICAN FOLKLORE SOCIETY

Bennett Hall - University of Pennsylvania, Philadelphia 4, Pennsylvania

MEMOIRS

James Teit. Traditions of the Thompson River Indians of British Columbia. With introduction by Franz Boas. 1898. 137 pp. $3.50.

George A. Dorsey. Traditions of the Skidi Pawnee. 1904. 366 pp. $4.

J.A. Teit, M.K. Gould, L. Farrand, and H.J. Spinden. Folk-Tales of Salishan and Sahaptin Tribes. 1917. 201 pp. $3.50.

Elsie Clews Parson. Tewa Tales. 1926. 304 pp. $3.50.

Elsie Clews Parson. Kiowa Tales. 1929. 152 pp. $2.50

Franz Boas. Bella Bella Tales. 1932. 178 pp. $3.50.

Thelma Adamson. Folk-Tales of the Coast Salish. 1943. 430 pp. $3.50.

Franz Boas. Kwakiutl Culture as Reflected Mythology. 1935. 190 pp. $3.

Morris Edward Opler. Myths and Tales of the Jicarilla Apache Indians. 1938. 406 pp. $3.50.

Martha W. Beckwith. Mandan-Hidatsa Myths and Ceremonies. 1938. 327 pp. $3.50.

Grenville Goodwin. Myths and Tales of the White Mountain Apache. 1939. 223 pp.

Elsie Clews Parsons. Taos Tales. 1940. 185 pp. $3.50.

Morris Edward Opler. Myths and Legends of the Lipan Apache Indians. 1940. 296 pp. $3.50.

Alfred Métraux. Myths and Tales of the Toba and Pilaga Indians of the Gran Chaco. 1946. 167 pp. $3.

Gladys Reichard. An Analysis of Coeur D'Alene Indian Myths. 1947. 218 pp. $3.

Katherine Spencer. Mythology and Values: An Analysis of Navaho Chantway Myths. 1957. 240 pp. $3.50; members' price $2.50.

Abenaki. 1901, 160; 1902, 62-3;
1912, 188-90.
Achomawi. 1908, 159-77;
1909, 283-7; 1931, 125-36.
Acoma. 1902, 88-90; 1918, 216f;
1930, 59-87.
Alaskan Tribes. 1888, 215;
1892, 232-5(Southern);
16-31, 85-103 (Kodiak
Island).
Agawam. 1907, 86-7.
Aleut. 1905, 215-22; 1907, 132f.;
1909, 10-24; 1947, 62f.
Algonquian (See specific tribes).
1891, 193-213; 1894, 201-04;
1898, 195-202; 1905, 185f.;
1914, 97 (Central); 1947, 259-64.
Apache (See Jicarilla, Mescalero).
1890, 209-12; 1898, 253-71;
1921, 319-20 (see Mohave);
1941, 10-23; 1946, 268-81.
Arapaho. 1912, 43-50
Arikara. 1909, 90-2.
Assiniboine. 1892, 72-3.
Athabascan (See specific tribes).
1900, 11-18; 1903, 180-5;
1908, 33-4; 1915, 207f.
Atlantic Coast Tribes. 1897, 243-4.
Atsugeqi. 1908, 159-177.

Biloxi. 1893, 48-50.
Blackfoot. 1890, 296-8; 1893, 44-7,
165-72; 1923, 401-03.
Bungee. 1906, 334-40.

Cahuilla. 1908, 239-40.
California (See specific tribes).
1892, 73-4; 1902, 104 (San
Joaquin Valley); 1906, 141f.;
1929, 307.
Canadian Tribes. 1894, 253
(Eastern); 1926, 450-9 (Northern);
1942, 1-18 (Middle Fraser River).
Carrier. 1934, 97-257.
Catawba. 1913, 319; 1947, 79-84.
Chemehuevi. 1908, 240-1.

Cherokee. 1892, 125-6; 1919, 391-3.
Cheyenne. 1900, 161-90; 1903, 108-15,
128; 1907, 169-94; 1908, 269-320;
1916, 406-08; 1921, 308-15.
Chickasaw. 1913, 292.
Chinook. 1893, 39-43; 1952, 121-9;
1953, 69-70 (Wasco).
Chipewyans. 1903, 73-4, 128.
Chitimacha. 1917, 474-8.
Chuh. 1915, 353.
Comanche. 1909, 273-82.
Coos. 1909, 25-41; 1949, 64-5.
Cree. 1897, 1-8; 1905, 139-43; 1916,
341-67 (Plains); 1921, 320 (Plains);
1923, 404-06; 1929, 309-53; 1953,
309-31.
Creek, 1954, 79-81.

Delaware. See Lenape.
Diegueños. 1901, 181-5; 1904, 217-40;
1908, 236.

Eskimo. 1889, 123-31; 1894, 45-50,
205-07, 209-13; 1897, 109-15;
1899, 19, 166-82; 1907, 296-9;
1909, 10-24; 1926, 79-81; 1954, 65f.

Flathead. 1901, 240-51; 1952, 359-60.
Fox. See Sauk-Fox.

Gay Head Tribes. 1898, 162.

Haida. 1889, 255; 1892, 43-7.
Hidatsa. 1912, 93-4.
Hoh. 1933, 297-346
Hopi (See Moki and specific tribes).
1929, 1-72; 1936, 1-68; 1948, 31f.
Hupa. 1948, 345-55.
Huron 1888, 177-83; 1889, 249-54;
1891, 289-94; 1899, 116f.; 1915, 83-95.

Iowa. 1925, 425-506.
Iroquois (See specific tribes). 1891,
295-306; 1892, 223-9; 1897, 169-80;
1898, 195-202; 1901, 153-5; 1910,
474-7.
Isleta. 1926, 70-8.

Joshua. 1915, 207f.

155